API DEVELOPMENT

A PRACTICAL GUIDE FOR BUSINESS IMPLEMENTATION SUCCESS

Sascha Preibisch

ca technologies

CA Press

Apress®

API Development: A Practical Guide for Business Implementation Success

Sascha Preibisch
Richmond, BC, Canada

ISBN-13 (pbk): 978-1-4842-4139-4   ISBN-13 (electronic): 978-1-4842-4140-0
https://doi.org/10.1007/978-1-4842-4140-0

Library of Congress Control Number: 2018963113

Managing Director, Apress Media LLC: Welmoed Spahr
Acquisitions Editor: Susan McDermott
Development Editor: Laura Berendson
Coordinating Editor: Rita Fernando

Distributed to the book trade worldwide by Springer Science+Business Media New York, 233 Spring Street, 6th Floor, New York, NY 10013. Phone 1-800-SPRINGER, fax (201) 348-4505, e-mail orders-ny@springer-sbm.com, or visit www.springeronline.com. Apress Media, LLC is a California LLC and the sole member (owner) is Springer Science + Business Media Finance Inc (SSBM Finance Inc). SSBM Finance Inc is a **Delaware** corporation.

For information on translations, please e-mail rights@apress.com, or visit www.apress.com/rights-permissions.

Apress titles may be purchased in bulk for academic, corporate, or promotional use. eBook versions and licenses are also available for most titles. For more information, reference our Print and eBook Bulk Sales web page at www.apress.com/bulk-sales.

Any source code or other supplementary material referenced by the author in this book is available to readers on GitHub via the book's product page, located at www.apress.com/9781484241394. For more detailed information, please visit www.apress.com/source-code.

Printed on acid-free paper

This book is for my mother and father who both are in heaven!

Contents

About the Author

 **Sascha Preibisch** has been involved in enterprise-grade software development since 2005. He worked as a consultant in Switzerland where he helped customers expose SOAP-based web services in a secure way. Today, as software architect for CA Technologies in Vancouver, Canada, he works with customers who expose RESTful services. He advises customers in the usage of OAuth, OpenID Connect, mobile API security, and SSO between mobile and desktop applications. Sascha regularly attends the Internet Identity Workshop (IIW) in Mountain View, California, USA, which is the birthplace of OAuth 2.0 and OpenID Connect. He is a member of the OpenID Foundation. He maintains a blog on all aspects of API development, and he wrote a short book about a software framework (*Application Development with XML, Eclipse RCP, and Web Services*). Sascha holds a patent on a secure mobile app registration protocol.

Please feel free to contact the author either via his professional blog space at https://communities.ca.com/blogs/oauth or via his personal web site at https://oauth.blog.

About the Technical Reviewer

Ola Mogstad is Engineering Director of the CA API Gateway development team in Vancouver, Canada and has spent the past 10+ years creating enterprise-grade software. He is a sci-fi and pizza enthusiast. Ola holds a Master's degree in Communication Technology from the Norwegian University of Science and Technology (NTNU).

Acknowledgments

First of all, I would like to thank my wife, Kerstin, and my two sons, Emil and Billy. They did not see me a lot while I wrote this book, but they continued to recognize me as member of our family and they supported me as much as they could!

Thanks to my employer, CA Technologies, for supporting me at every step in the writing process.

Special thanks to Ola Mogstad, Victor Kazakov, Evgenia Pshenichnova, Jack Cha, David Young, Jay Thorne, Scott Morrison, Matt McLarty and Mike Bibblecombe for their reviews, feedback, and technical guidance.

Introduction

This book is about application programming interfaces (APIs) that provide access to enterprise systems. This book is meant for anyone who is involved in API-based projects. The book discusses general design guidelines, talks about relevant stakeholders, explains the difference between client- and server-side APIs, provides implementation details independent of programming languages, and explains the concept of microservices. Most of the content is based on use cases of enterprise businesses. The book finds itself in the category of *practical/useful* rather than *theoretically explained*.

The book addresses different audiences and has high-level sections just as very technical ones. If you are in the process of exposing business data via APIs, consider this book to be part of your decision-making process. If this is the first time you are going through the process of creating APIs, or the first time since the days of SOAP services, there is a high chance that you will find answers to your questions here.

This book is also about phrases and terms that are used in the context of APIs and should help different audiences communicate with each other on the same level.

From a technical point of view, this book concentrates on HTTP-based APIs that leverage OAuth 2.0, OpenID Connect, JSON Web Token (JWT), and RESTful interfaces. These technologies will be discussed in detail. The book also introduces microservice architectures and how Docker comes into play. Deep technical knowledge is generally not required.

On a side note, please be aware that this book is not written in a gender or otherwise neutral language. Please assume it is referencing persons in general.

Why I Wrote This Book

Almost from the first day of my career in IT I have been involved in the API business. As a consultant in Switzerland, I worked for big companies. These companies mainly integrated their systems with other equally big businesses. The systems usually exchanged SOAP messages and supported use cases such as transmitting pay stubs or health insurance reports. You may remember those days and may still have to support those solutions.

Now, as a software architect, I am mainly involved in API projects that use RESTful interfaces. My involvement is requested to discuss architectural questions. At some point, I realized that those questions were very similar to each other. At that point in time, I decided to start a blog to talk about topics in the context of APIs. Some of my posts have 100 views, others a few thousand, which is a lot in my personal world. Seeing those numbers indicated to me that my posts matched what people were looking for.

Based on that, a few months ago colleagues suggested I write a book based on topics from my blog but with more details and written for different audiences. I thought about it, I liked the idea, and now I am sitting here night after night writing this book whereas my colleagues are enjoying time with their families!

However, I am very excited and happy to share my experiences with anyone involved in the process of exposing APIs. If at least one person can say *This book is just what I was looking for*, it would be a huge success and the main reason why I wrote this book!

APIs: What Are They?

There are many kinds and types of application programming interfaces (APIs). This book will only concentrate on a short list of them and this chapter is meant to get everyone on the same page.

What Is Understood as an API

Let me start with a statement that concentrates on the *I* of API, which, at least for me, is the most important piece:

An interface is a well-defined entry point into a system.

Here are a few examples of interfaces in different contexts:

- **An electrical socket**: There is a socket and a plug. The plug goes into the socket, and the device connected to the socket works.

- **A vending machine**: You put money into the machine, you select the desired item, and the machine issues the item.

- **A helicopter**: You pull the pitch and the helicopter takes off. You push the stick into any direction and the helicopter follows it.

© CA 2018
S. Preibisch, *API Development*, https://doi.org/10.1007/978-1-4842-4140-0_1

These examples have one thing in common: they expose very complex systems in a relatively simple and easy-to-use form. Using a plug with a socket is extremely easy. Very little knowledge is required to use it. However, this is only true because the complexity behind it is hidden. You do not need to know where the electricity comes from and you do not need to know how the electricity is delivered to this one specific socket. You just need to match the style of plug and socket, and off you go.

The story around the helicopter is a little different. Most of you have not flown a helicopter but can still imagine that it is not a simple task. (I can assure you, it is not! I flew a Westland Sea King Mk 41 in a simulator during my time in the military and crashed it even after a successful landing!) The nearest machine to a helicopter that most people have controlled is most likely a drone. They behave similarly to helicopters but can often be steered using a mobile phone or tablet. It is difficult to imagine a simpler way of controlling a flying vehicle than that.

Nevertheless, I stick to my statement that the interface for flying a helicopter is very simple, only that "simple" is relative and is true for skilled users! And this brings me to one of my favorite sayings:

A fool with a tool is still a fool!

Full credit for that goes to my former colleague Niels, who brought that saying from San Francisco back to Switzerland. The message is simple: tools and interfaces only help skilled users!

Now let's add the *AP* of API: *application programming* interface. You all know some kind of API. Whether within a programming language or a protocol or a web site, you have used some sort of API. By looking at *application programming interfaces*, you have left the world of *simple* interfaces. If you do not agree, you have not seen many APIs. Before you disagree, let me share my favorite image (Figure 1-1) on that topic with you, which is based on an image created by Eric Burke.

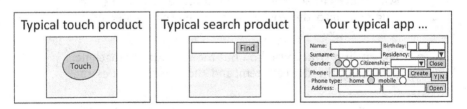

Figure 1-1. Simple-to-use devices and applications ... and your own

If you have designed APIs for one of the first two UIs,[1] I apologize, and you may stop reading now. If you are an expert on the APIs behind the third UI, I welcome you to continue reading.

Many developers believe a simple user interface is the result of great web design. Please note: they are most likely wrong. Simple user interfaces have very strong APIs behind them. Here is an example: when I attended my favorite workshop, IIW[2] in Mountain View, California, Google gave a presentation on the topic of user authentication. To summarize it, the very simple login screen is powered by a system of 30 or more individual components and their APIs! These APIs are fed by the content of the search field and hidden values in the browser that are not visible to users and do not need manual input. Users do not even need to know that they exist!

Designing simple user interfaces is not an easy task. Developers of different areas with different expertise have to come together to make it happen. However, we will ignore UI-related tasks behind the user interface since this book is concentrating on server-side APIs. To get closer to explaining *what is understood as an API*, I will reference the user interfaces shown in Figure 1-1.

The example shows a user interface on the right side with many input fields, check boxes, and radio buttons—practically all UI elements are used. All of those elements are required because the UI is nothing more than a collector of data, which is required by an existing server API. Ending up with such a user interface could have several reasons: the server API needs the data to create an account, but no user context was available so nothing could have been prefilled or preselected. Developers felt it was the fasted and easiest way for them to implement it. Product owners could mistakenly believe that users need their system and therefore do not have a choice anyways.

Whatever happens, try to put yourself into the user's shoes. Always consult UX experts who may be able to help with revisiting the design of your server APIs. You could support default values, you could implement server APIs that do not need all data at once, and you could implement a multistep flow that eases the use of your system.

In comparison, the simple user interfaces were built on top of well-designed and architected API systems. A possible approach to get there may have been a UI-first approach: design the UI and then design the APIs to support it! Similar, but not completely the same: the aircraft Fairchild Republic A-10 Thunderbolt II was designed around a tank cracking gun. Also, electric-first cars are designed around electric drive systems. In general, design what is important first but do not try to squeeze *the square peg into a round hole*!

---

[1]UI, user interface
[2]IIW, Internet Identity Workshop, www.internetidentityworkshop.com

In regards to API systems, I would like to clarify the distinction between client- and server-side APIs. I will describe the difference using an image that represents a simple application. The goal of the application is to display a catalog of some sort to a user of a mobile app. The high-level flow is as follows:

1. User clicks the "Display Catalog" button.

2. The mobile app executes the client-side API named getCatalog().

3. getCatalog() calls the external server-side API named https://server.external.com/mobile/catalog.

4. That API calls the internal server API named https://server.internal.com/catalog?type=mobile.

5. That API selects data from a database and transforms it into a mobile app-friendly response.

This system will not appear out of nowhere nor will it function by accident. Many things must be considered and must work together, and they must be especially designed to do so. Take a look at Figure 1-2. It contains different boxes representing a client or a server and also shows pseudo code.

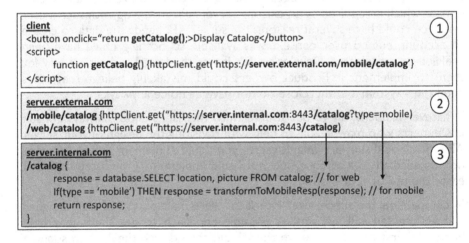

Figure 1-2. Client-side vs. server-side APIs

As my former manager Jay would say, *Let me explain*:

Box 1: The Client

A product owner wants a mobile app that displays a catalog. An app developer implements the screen to be shown. A **client-side API developer** provides a library (<script> .... </script>) with an **API** (function) , getCatalog().

This enables the app developer to create a sexy UI and the one and only thing he has to do is execute getCatalog() that spits out exactly what he needs. The app developer does not need to know what happens behind the scenes, which simplifies his life as a developer. He can concentrate on building delightful screens.

Box 2: The External Server

That server exposes two **external server-side APIs**: /mobile/catalog and /web/catalog. These two APIs receive requests from mobile (as in this example) or web clients. The main task is to validate and forward these requests to the internal catalog API. As you can see, there is only one internal server side API, /catalog. It will be called with a query parameter (?type=mobile) to give a hint of the expected type of response. It may not be obvious, but these two APIs also help simplifying the mobile app/client API developer's lives. Sending the query parameter ?type=mobile is not required for them. This is handled in the API /mobile/catalog.

Box 3: The Internal Server

The internal server exposes the **internal server-side API**, /catalog, which does all the work: it finds data from the database and creates a response matching the expectations of the client (either mobile or web).

Overall, each API was designed to simplify someone else's life and to support this use case. To sum it up, here are highlights you want to remember:

- A client-side API hides the complexity that is involved in managing requests to servers. SDKs[3] are good examples of such API providers. A client-side API named registerApp() may register an application on a server. The registerApp() API (function) provided by an SDK may execute complicated tasks such as generating a CSR, extracting device details, managing user sessions, and sending and receiving requests and responses from servers. One single client-side API will often interact with one or multiple server-side APIs.

- A server-side API exposes a well-defined entry point into and out of a closed system. There may be multiple APIs for the same purpose but for different types of clients. An API named /register may require five input parameters for clients that can provide application details, user details, and device details. The API /register/client may accept three parameters only if no user context is available. The latter API could add default values to compensate the missing user context but use the same registration backend as the first API.

---

[3]SDK, software development kit

I hope the difference between **client-side** and **server-side** APIs is now tangible.

With all that said, I would like to conclude this section with slightly different explanations of *what is understood as an API* then you would find at other locations:

- An API is an enabler for business opportunities.

- An API indicates how much users are appreciated.

- An API indicates how much developers are engaged.

Nothing more, nothing less!

What Types of APIs Exist?

After reading this section you may be surprised to find types of APIs that you are aware off but have not been mentioned. Do not be surprised, please. This book is based on my own experiences and therefore any list cannot be considered as *complete*. It may also happen that you do not even agree on what I consider to be a *type* of API. In the end, I still hope that you get something to take with you.

From my point of view, an API has nothing to do with technology, at least not on a higher level. I once worked for a company that developed catalog creation/printing software. Their product was based on C++ but over time it also included Java. At some point, the CTO required every API to be available in both languages so that a developer could use her preferred programming language during product development. You could argue one API was of type C++, the other of type *Java*. I would argue it had nothing to do with type. No matter if it was used with C++ or Java, the usage was the same and the input and output was the same; it was just made for specific programming languages.

With that in mind, I can identify two different categories for APIs: use case and intended consumer. Here are examples for the category of use case:

- **Finance**: Banks, credit cards, debt collectors, financial services

- **Health**: Doctors, hospitals

- **Insurance**: Car, tenant, life

- **Gaming**: Online gaming

- **Government**: Public services

- **Shopping**: Including mobile services, electronics, tools, foods

- **Logistics**: Managing goods transportation in general

I like the categorization by use case since almost all companies can assign themselves to at least one of them. The advantage is that regulations, best practices, specifications, RFCs,[4] or laws are in place that should or have to be respected. Being able to approach types of APIs this way takes you half way to your requirements document without reinventing the wheel.

Let's say your company assigns itself to the category *Finance*. You do not have to search very long to find specifications you may want to or must follow:

- **PCI**: Payment Card Industry security standards. If your system handles any credit card-based transactions, you must be PCI-compliant.

- **FIPS 140**: Federal Information Processing Standard, publication 1 and 2 (FIPS 140-1, FIPS 140-2). Issued by NIST[5]. Applies if cryptography is required, which is the case for financial institutions.

- **PSD2**: Payment Service Directive 2. A European directive to force financial institutions to create APIs for accessing account information (high level). This is required for European institutions but should also be considered outside of Europe.

- **FAPI**: Financial-grade APIs by OpenID Foundation. A list of typical requirements to support financial tasks such as checking account information and transferring funds between accounts via APIs. Meant as a guideline for any company that has to adhere to PSD2.

While talking about types of APIs, I would like to remind you that you should **never categorize** them **by their visibility** such as "private" and "public." What I mean by that is the concept of calling an API private only because it is not publicly documented or publicly introduced otherwise. It has been shown that any kind of API will be *found* by someone and then misused. Even if you are exposing APIs for private consumption, you should always treat them as if they had been made publicly available! Assuming you are *safe* since your API is *private* may lower your standards in regards to authentication and authorization, rate limiting, and sanitizing content that gets exposed.

After reading about a "breach" of your very own system in the press, you will find yourself in your company's head office having a chat with your CEO—the type of chat you may have had during school time with your principal when he was not amused with you!

---

[4]RFC, Request For Comments, www.ietf.org/standards/rfcs/
[5]NIST, National Institute of Standards and Technology, www.nist.gov

Here are examples for the category of intended consumer:

- **B2C**: Business-to-consumer
- **B2B**: Business-to-business

The categorization by intended consumer helps you to get a feeling for the number of expected users and with that an expected traffic volume. For example, if you are a mobile service provider, you may have 10, 20, or 50 million customers. Potentially each one will download your app to access their private information, which is located in your data center. This is a very different story than having a business partner with 500 users. Here are a few assumptions you can derive from knowing your intended audience:

- **Type B2C**: Leverage an OAuth (RFC 6749) and OpenID Connect (http://openid.net/connect) infrastructure. These protocols cover authentication, authorization, and resource API protection. Guidelines for mobile app development (RFC 8252) exist. OpenID Certified providers (cloud and on-premises) already exist and can be considered (http://openid.net/certification/). You can calculate the concurrent sessions you need to handle and with that you can lay out the required infrastructure.

- **Type B2B**: Leverage an OAuth and OpenID Connect infrastructure or use SAML for federated user authentication and authorization. SAML (https://en.wikipedia.org/wiki/SAML/_2.0) is well supported.

The type B2C has some non-functional requirements that also apply to the type B2B, but are more important here. Whereas business partners are active during working hours, Monday - Friday, consumers are active 24/7. Let's have a look at the consequences:

- **Support**: Your support team needs to be available 24/7. That team needs to have at least one expert per system component. You may even need to include engineers to be available on-demand.

- **Redundancy**: Your system needs to have redundant system components. And it is important to pay attention to details. Here is an example: if your system requires a web server, you need two of them. If any web application running on that server needs a database, you need two of them, too! It may sound obvious, but I have seen it all.

- **CI/CD**: You need to have a CI/CD chain that allows you to update your system at any given time. The CI/CD chain needs to be automated, not scripted! Especially with redundant components updates cannot be applied manually. Otherwise, sooner or later, your components will run different versions of the same software and escalations will be unavoidable.

Summary

It is important for every project to clearly understand which type of API needs to be supported. Knowing this guides the project in the correct direction. Many requirements can be derived from that information. After reading this chapter, all involved persons should be on the same page or at least know which questions to ask before going ahead.

API Stake-holders

Any organization has different teams involved in every project. Some projects may require teams that handle internal network traffic; other projects may need external network traffic teams. Topics, such as authentication or authorization, may involve different teams than mobile app development. But in some cases, members of almost all teams are required. Exposing business data via APIs is one of those cases.

The following is a list of roles that are required and referenced in this book. You may hope not to find your own role listed, but that wish will not come true, especially since you are reading this book.

Product Owners

A product owner is the person who has an idea for a feature that requires external-facing APIs. She is the one who convinces the business that her idea will drive revenue and will be an overall enhancement. She may even be able to identify different user groups that are looking forward to the new API-based features. Of all involved roles she has the luxury of not needing to know how the technology behind it works, just like sales persons who promise features based on alpha-release demos and leave it up to engineers to make it happen after these features have been sold. Product owners cannot totally ignore technology, though; they have to work closely with engineers. Exposing features via an API has limitations and tradeoffs everyone must be aware off to avoid unrealistic expectations.

© CA 2018
S. Preibisch, *API Development*, https://doi.org/10.1007/978-1-4842-4140-0_2

These are tasks product owners should own based on their responsibilities:

- Specify what an API-based feature or product should do.
- Specify how and by whom the system should be consumed.
- Specify what type of data to capture.
- Do not dictate implementation details or technologies.
- Become a user of your system! Doing so is the best way for identifying potential areas for improvement.
- Own the roadmap and be excited about it! This may sound obvious, but I have seen many cases where product owners asked developers, *Ok, what do you think we need next?* This is not generally terrible, but it should not be the main approach for finding new ideas. Engineers will typically come up with great *technical* ideas but not necessarily *business-relevant* ones.

Software Architects

Some time ago I spoke to another parent while we were watching our children play a soccer game. We spoke about work life and ended up talking about my role of software architect. She said, *You are an architect? That is a tough job!* I don't think it is, but it was interesting to hear her comment. If your role is a software architect too, take a moment to reflect on it. As an architect, you know exactly how things should work. But you have to deal with product owners, engineers, operations, and other people who are not involved but have an opinion. You have to deal with compromises, lack of knowledge, and new technologies that you may have missed. And yet we are the ones being blamed or celebrated. Nevertheless, for your own benefit, look at the product or the overall system you are responsible for and how satisfied users are right now. I hope you are happy with what you have achieved so far. Enjoy it, an API project may change that!

API-based systems are quite different than "simple" software products and have other challenges. Anything you design needs to leverage and provide API interfaces, in many cases HTTP-based ones. Not having Java or C# or PHP classes communicating with each other, but stateless HTTP network calls requires a different mindset. It is not about class A talking to class B to implement interface C. There are no classes, there are no programming languages, there are no compilers finding issues in code, and there are no deep integrations. The only thing that exists are requests where the previous one has nothing to do with the current one. Request and response parameters, that's it, more or less. With that in mind, try to approach architecture from a different angle and be open to going down new paths.

Let's look at a simple example. You may have designed an authentication service in the past that was implemented with a few classes and interfaces, as illustrated in Figure 2-1 (as an architect you would usually design something bigger, but this is meant to illustrate the situation). The system consists of an LDAP (Lightweight Directory Access Protocol) server that is leveraged by an IDP (Identity Provider). Together they provide access to the details of users. If you are not familiar with this concept, here is an example: when you authenticate on your work computer, your employee is the IDP and your user credentials are found within an LDAP server.

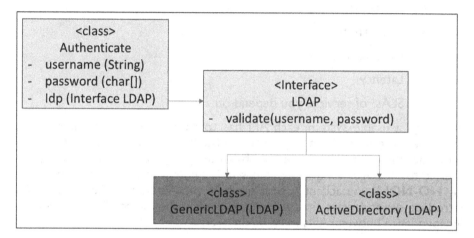

Figure 2-1. View of a simple authentication service. (ActiveDirectory is often referenced as AD.)

Pretty straightforward, nothing to worry about. But now, let's compare it with the API-based solution shown in Figure 2-2.

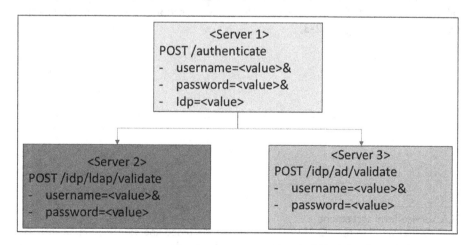

Figure 2-2. View of a simple API-based authentication service

There is no class diagram anymore. There is a diagram showing different servers supporting multiple APIs (i.e. /authenticate, /idp/ldap/validate). Server1 receives HTTP POST requests and sends a request to Server2 or Server3. Server2 and Server3 validate the given credentials and respond with an error or success message. With this system you now have to deal with completely different obstacles:

- Timeouts
- Network zones
- Authentication
- Authorization
- Message sizes
- Latency
- SLAs[1] of services you depend on

To design a usable system, each API has to specify for itself what it does and how it can be consumed. A typical mistake is to introduce assumptions on whom the API will be consumed by. In design meetings you should react allergic to messages such as *API 1 has to integrate with Client XYZ*. That is a big **NO-NO**! If you accept special treatment for dedicated clients, you will introduce dependencies that will cause issues in the future. The concept of independence between APIs must be protected.

However, you will still be asked to support Client XYZ differently than others. One way for you to get out of the dilemma is to extend the API. If your general requirement for authentication requires *username, password* you may be able to accept a *JWT*[2] too if that is what Client XYZ can provide. As long as the JWT validation itself has no dependency on Client XYZ and if JWT validation is an added value for your API anyways, it could be a viable approach. It would look like Figure 2-3.

---

[1]SLA, service-level agreement
[2]JWT, JSON Web Token, RFC 7519. These will be discussed and explained in Chapter 5. For now, consider them a digitally signed single sign-on token.

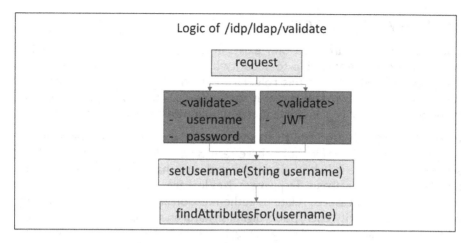

Figure 2-3. View of extended API

Your API receives credentials, validates them, sets a username, and finds attributes for the user. You could go wild now and build those two types of credential validation within their own APIs. The only limits are available resources and all obstacles listed above!

These are tasks software architects should own based on their responsibilities:

- Specify the APIs. They are the pillars of the system!

- Specify the role each involved component in the system takes on and identify owners.

- Identify owners of dependent, external components and request SLAs for each one.

- Delegate the design of smaller components but review them.

- Be critical and do not accept any changes without convincing reasons and a chain of decision-making artifacts, not to blame others in the future but to review what caused the changes. This may help improve the process for future projects.

- Do not try to be everyone's friend but be the friend of the systems users. (Why? You have to be the one standing as firm as a rock between users and a bad system!)

- Do not dictate implementation details. Make suggestions only! In a world of APIs, you may not even need to know which programming languages are used for different API implementations.

Security Architects

The role of security architect only exists in rare cases and only in companies that have a deep relationship to security by design. In most cases, one or a few engineers will take on this role. However, the role is explained with its tasks, not necessarily meaning that it has to be occupied by a specific person. Nevertheless, security is important and should never be underestimated.

External-facing APIs are used to expose internal data. If a company is in the research business, it may want to share results with the entire world as a free service or monetize it. In both cases, the goal is to share very specific data and not the complete database. To prevent data leakage, APIs must apply security measures. These measures relate to authentication and authorization, auditing, network-level security, encryption, digital signatures, number of datasets, times when data is available, not distinguishing between internal and external users, and more. The role that is responsible for specifying these measures is the security architect. If that role is yours, please remember this: **Your failures may end up in the news!**

You, as a security architect, may not be responsible for the API design directly. But you will still be blamed if the API exposes unauthorized data. Your task is to define rules and guidelines and checklists that API developers must follow. Below are a few typical cases for which you must develop guidelines. The list is quite specific since it includes implementation details such as demanding OAuth. To include those details or not depends on the type of guideline or documentation and should be used as an inspiration.

- **APIs for sharing personal data**: Prevent any unauthorized client or user from retrieving data. Use OAuth 2.0 and OpenID Connect.

- **APIs accepting federated users**: Prevent unauthorized third-party users from accessing the API. Use SAML[3] or OpenID Connect for that. Both technologies allow the API to leverage digital signatures for validation purposes.

- **APIs accessed anonymously**: Even if an API is open to any user, apply rate limitations and require TLS[4] and an ApiKey[5]. The goal is to audit the used application and prevent the backend system from being overloaded.

- If APIs are used with HTTP, **always** require HTTPS. Plain HTTP should be an exception!

---

[3]Security Assertion Markup Language, https://tools.ietf.org/html/rfc7522
[4]Transport Layer Security, https://tools.ietf.org/html/rfc5246
[5]ApiKey identifies an application

A very important aspect, but sometimes underrated, is auditing. If audits do not capture interactions with a system, it is open for fraud. On the other hand, if all interactions on all levels of the application are audited, it will most likely perform badly. You have to find the fine line between *what is required* and *what is overkill*. There is a nice comparison to be made with the world of machinery: **Design it to be as precise as needed and as inaccurate as possible.** An example of this is a specification stating that a tolerance of 0.1 mm is good enough, although 0.05 mm could be achieved.

Here is an example where auditing was missing: I used to blog on a platform that had different logical locations to group content for different audiences. At some point, one of my blog posts was moved from my personal blog space to a different one. In addition, I also lost all privileges on it so that I could not modify or move it back. As it turned out, the system administrator was not able to find any details about that event in the auditing system. He did move it back manually and promised to take action to prevent such magical movements. (If you have seen something like this in your system, you should stop reading and talk to your product owner right now!) Just imagine if this was a banking system where a transaction got executed without leaving any trace!

No matter what, as a security architect you should require all types of events to be audited that you believe are necessary to secure your system, even if it turns out that it is impossible to support them. There may still be a valuable compromise between your requirements and preventing the system from being usable.

These are tasks security architects should own based on their responsibilities:

- Specify requirements for auditing. Imagine the case where you need to track the lifecycle of individual requests. When was it received, when was the response created, and what happened when and where in between?

- Specify when and where authentication and authorization are required. This depends on requirements per API, which makes it challenging. Nevertheless, these are two important topics.

- Specify network-level authentication and authorization requirements.

API Developers

There are many types of APIs and therefore there are many types of API developers. If you talk to a member of the mobile app development team, you may hear him say, *Our SDK exposes APIs that we have developed.* Same thing if you talk to members of the API Gateway team: *We have developed APIs that expose features to external clients.* This is a brief explanation on the type of API developers handled in this section and in this book generally:

- API developers who expose APIs to the **external** network
- API developers who expose APIs to the **internal** network

All other API developers are certainly welcome, but the focus is on the ones above. If you ask me for the reason, it is very simple: it is my expertise, I am a server guy. More importantly, though, this book is focused on securing APIs that expose business data. That is not done by a mobile app SDK. *But Sascha, our SDK API exposes business data, too!* Yes, I know. But this SDK API is constrained by the external server API. And that external API is constrained by the internal API. I envision it as a stream of data that gets weaker the further away it gets from its origin. Figure 2-4 illustrates this.

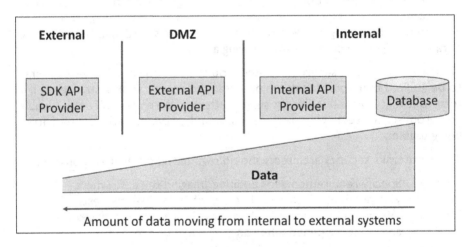

Figure 2-4. Reducing amount of exposed data when moving from internal to external network areas

Now that you know who this section is focusing on, and if this is your role, let's put some pressure on you. If you are hindering **API adoption** through bad design, you are the one to be blamed; no one else! It is your responsibility to delight your customers with a well-designed API. No matter what, if your API is cumbersome, nobody will use it. All other aspects of your implementation will be relatively less important when it comes to adoption. Third-party developers will not consider your offering and internal developers will find other solutions. An internal discussion will probably start like this:

The provided APIs are very sophisticated. Unfortunately, our use case is very different so we have decided to develop our own solution.

In other words:

What were they thinking? The APIs are not even remotely usable!

As an API developer, you will face many challenges. Big ones! Some of them are created by your very own colleagues. The magic word is **requirements**. Your security architect, client-side developers, business owners, backend developers, and maybe even third-party partners all have requirements for you. And many of those requirements will conflict with each other. If you accept them all, you will miss timelines, your API will be difficult to use, it will be too restrictive, it will perform badly, and it will be very difficult to maintain.

To survive this situation, you have to learn to filter out necessary and important requirements from those that fit into the category of *nice to have, later.* If you do not do that, you will be the one having to explain to your boss' boss why the months (or years) of the long and very expensive API project only produced a mess. Another side effect of not being able to say **no** is you will see things you may not have seen for a while: **stars in the night sky**. The reason is very simple: you will be the one taking the night shift, working on escalations in your production system. I know because it happened to me!

These are tasks API developers should own based on their responsibilities:

- The main goal is to support the business requirements made by the product owner.

- The second goal is to adhere to the given architecture and the provided security guidelines.

- Follow best practices for API implementations.

Other Roles

There are other roles and teams in an organization that I have not specifically called out. Documentation, QA, and Support are some of them. All these groups are involved in API projects and they are important. The only difference is that the former four groups are the ones sitting in the front row, they are the ones making most decisions, and they are also the ones called when escalations arise.

Needless to say, release parties have to include everyone!

Responsibilities

After reading this chapter, you should understand the four roles and their responsibilities. Nevertheless, I would like to stress that topic.

People often want to take on responsibilities that are not theirs. Sometimes they do it on purpose; sometimes they do not realize what they are doing. For example, a previous manager of mine delegated tasks to myself and other senior developers. However, he did not let go; he continued to take on those tasks himself. When I confronted him with this, he immediately said, *You are right, I will step back!* There is a big difference between delegating responsibilities and letting go of them. Always pay attention to this and reflect it yourself.

Taking on other team members' responsibilities has many drawbacks. I like to talk about my time as a rugby player to explain how ownership of responsibilities should work.

In rugby, there are 15 players, and each one is important. Each one takes on a very specific role and a very specific position on the field. A rugby game can only be won if all 15 members stick to their roles and positions. If a player gets dragged away, he should go back to his original position as soon as he can. The worst that can happen during a rugby game is players who ignore this rule. Positions will be left empty and others will be occupied twice. Having a position occupied twice is bad, but having positions empty is a catastrophe. Dependencies are broken, players are confused, players lose confidence in the team's organization, they lose their trust in other players and finally, they lose the game. Successful teams do not have this issue. Successful teams have players who own, who are accountable, and who respect others. (Take a peek at www.worldrugby.org/video/337898 and watch one of the best teams, the New Zealand All Blacks,[6] start winning the game even before it starts.)

If you apply this to software development, it is not that different. Each role is important, each role has to be owned, and there has to be a general trust among team members. In the end, everyone wants to win the game!

Unfortunately, this does not always seem work out. In comparison to rugby, organizations have hierarchical structures and some team members are more equal than others. Decision-making processes are often found outside of a specific team. Due to these circumstances, it is even more important to be very clear about who decides what and who is responsible for what. Never exclude owners in any email thread or other discussions. Always be accountable for your own piece of the pie.

During rugby games, there is a lot of shouting between players. During API projects, there needs to be a lot of shouting, too! Not for personal reasons, but for the sake of the project. Everyone involved has to be very critical. They must be able to ask *What was your decision-making process?* If those types of questions cause confusion or worse, an answer like *Not sure, just thought this may be the right thing to do...*, must raise your concerns!

---

[6]In this case, the U20 team. Even at their young age they are very impressive!

Ownership, accountability, reliability, and respect are the recipe for successful API projects!

If team members are clear about their responsibilities, own them, and are serious about them, the API project has a good chance of being successful. Understanding responsibilities is one of the very first and most important steps in any project.

Summary

An API project requires different roles to get involved and align their goals. It is important to adjust to each other early and respect boundaries. Too often teams believe that others know what they need or want, which is most likely not the case. It is better to state the obvious often than fail later. If the listed roles do not exist, they should be created, even as part-time jobs. Otherwise, certain views get neglected, which will cause trouble in the form of escalations further down the line.

Importance and Relevance of APIs

APIs are important from different points of views. The business looks at APIs from a revenue-driven angle whereas engineers see technical benefits. Arguments on both sides must be considered; both sides must understand each other's desires. This chapter gives an overview of the arguments on both sides.

The Business Value of APIs

Businesses look at APIs to reduce costs, open their system to a broader audience, or monetize services. Although I am an engineer, I do get involved in business-related discussions when I attend meetings with enterprise customers. Those discussions are usually driven by engineers who seek advice on how to leverage my company's product in order to satisfy business needs.

© CA 2018
S. Preibisch, *API Development*, https://doi.org/10.1007/978-1-4842-4140-0_3

My impression is that businesses are very well aware of the power APIs bring to the table. If done right, the business can grow, costs can be reduced, and new market opportunities can arise. Here are a few reasons why customers have introduced external- and internal-facing APIs from a business point of view:

- **Omnipresent**: Any user should be able to consume services at any point in time and from any kind of device.

- **Mobile first:** Similar as above but with a focus on being present in app stores. Even if it is just a simple app, they want their company's name to be found.

- **Integrations:** Enable easy user on-boarding and third-party systems integrations.

- **Modernization:** Understanding that times change and monolithic systems that use closed and undocumented interfaces are difficult to maintain, upgrade, replace, and support.

- **Automatization:** This may sound like a technical requirement, but businesses are aware that a modernized infrastructure can only be managed if processes, such as testing, upgrading, and deployments are automated. Automatization is possible only if APIs are available for those tasks.

- **Monetization:** Monetize the usage of APIs. Some businesses can provide data for which third-party developers are willing to pay.

Not a single item of above was mentioned by accident or without reasoning. Let me share the details for each one.

Omnipresent

The business requirement for "omnipresent" could be as simple as this: *Users need to be able to fulfill their needs within our application, independent of time and location.*

The interpretation could sound harmless and be communicated as such: *We need to provide a unified user experience across all online platforms, including mobile and desktop applications. The user's workflow should not be interrupted when switching apps or platforms.*

Before I explain the challenges associated with that, take a look at Figure 3-1.

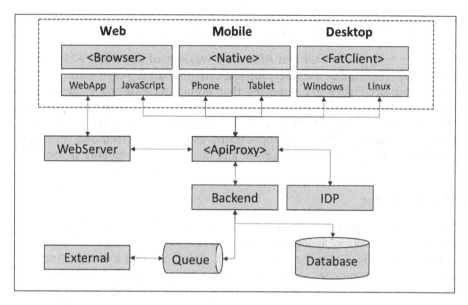

Figure 3-1. Components connected via APIs

"Omnipresent" references applications enclosed by the dotted lines. Everything within that square should be usable "as one" app and practically everywhere available. Here is an example use case: a user is on his daily commute home from work and opens an app on his mobile phone. He checks account details and realizes that he needs to update them. To do so, he opens the same app on his tablet and expects to be able to continue his work where he left it on the phone. Once he gets home, he turns on his desktop computer, opens the same application, and finishes the work.

If you are an engineer, you may have an idea of the challenges associated with this scenario. For everyone else, I will explain what those few sentences mean. Applications running on different platforms are implemented using different programming languages, often accompanied by proprietary protocols. For example, an application implemented for Windows cannot be installed on an Android platform. If it's about desktop applications only, existing technologies such as CORBA[1] can be leveraged in some cases, even though it is heavyweight and complicated. Unfortunately, that technology is not suitable for mobile applications.

On the other hand, if it's about mobile applications only, newer standards such as Bluetooth[2] and NFC[3] can help. Sadly, these two technologies are not generally available for applications installed on desktop computers. Running

---

[1]CORBA, Common Object Request Broker Architecture, www.corba.org
[2]Bluetooth, www.bluetooth.com
[3]NFC, Near-Field Communication, https://nfc-forum.org

out of options, a completely different solution, and then applications that communicate directly with each other, must be found.

Businesses have discovered that APIs are a way out of this issue. APIs enable indirect communication between applications, no matter which platform they are running on. Figure 3-1 indicates that communication via a component named ApiProxy (more details on it in Chapter 6). The ApiProxy provides RESTful APIs and all applications can leverage them. In combination with a protocol that specifies how applications can be addressed and messages exchanged, the problem can be solved and business requirements supported.

Mobile First

"Mobile first" expresses the desire to support mobile applications with a higher priority than desktop applications. Businesses are aware that users expect availability on any device, be it a phone, a tablet, or even a watch. Another association with mobile applications refers to geographical independency. Mobile applications are installed on devices that are carried around all over the globe. Independent of the current location, users expect their applications to be available and work just fine.

Mobile-first requirements are not only driven by businesses that provide online services. They also apply to hardware providers such as in cars, cameras, hi-fi systems, lights, washing machines, TVs, and many others. The availability of mobile applications in these areas becomes more and more relevant. There are multiple reasons for that, as far as I have understood it from customers. On one hand, users want their devices to be connected with systems such as Amazon Alexa and Google Home. On the other hand, third-party vendors want to provide services based on those abilities.

Businesses are aware that providing at least a simple and well working mobile application is often a minimum requirement to attract users, and with that, customers. Businesses are also aware that APIs are the only realistic way to support these apps. APIs become the enabler to get into the mobile application market and, with that, participation in markets such as house automation.

Integration

Integration is always a big topic. Businesses want to be able to integrate with other systems. They also want other systems to integrate with theirs. These cases do not only require a business to provide APIs for its own and potential third-party usage. It is also important to be able to leverage external third-party APIs. Otherwise, a one-directional system gets created, which does not surface all of the features that would be possible in a system supporting both directions, similar to a car that does not have a reverse gear. It will only take you so far before you get stuck!

Here are typical cases that have been brought up during discussions:

Easy on-boarding of new users. In many cases, this refers to social login, which is a process that enables users to reuse an existing social platform account (such as an existing Gmail address) for creating a local account in the business' system. This feature is purely driven through bidirectional API integrations. Businesses know that a missing "... or use your existing xyz-platform account ..." button on their web site or their mobile app may cost them potential new users. Having to create yet another username/password-based account is not an acceptable process for many users.

In other cases, easy on-boarding refers to the process of users switching apps or devices. Let's say a user logged into the system using social login; he now has a session within the businesses system. If the same user opens a second app, his expectation is to reuse the existing session. In other words, he should *automagically* be logged in. A similar expectation can be observed when opening the same app on a different device. Here's an example: my 10-year-old son used to play a game on my wife's phone. One day, he got his own phone. When I told him we now have to find out how to transfer his gaming data to his phone, he answered, *Dad, just place the phones next to each other and the data will move over.*

The last case of easy on-boarding involves different platforms. It's the same idea as above, but in this case, users want to seamlessly switch from mobile apps to web applications on their desktops. Many of you may have seen this feature with WhatsApp[4] or WeChat.[5] These mobile applications allow users to extend their sessions to web applications by simply scanning a QR code[6] using their mobile app. Nothing else is required. With that, switching from the mobile app to the web application only takes one click!

All these scenarios are API driven!

Do it all here use cases. Businesses do not want users to leave their application due to what I call "missing completeness." I refer to "completeness" like this:

Enable users to complete all their needs within one application!

Businesses are usually aware of their competitors. They are also aware that the quality of their own online services may be one of very few differentiators. Here is an example.

The fictional company *SaschasSlowPackages* is in the business of moving packages from A to B. This company provides a mobile application with just one feature, tracking packages. Other information, such as store locations, office hours, package prices, is available on a static web site only. This mobile

---

[4]WhatsApp, www.whatsapp.com
[5]WeChat, https://web.wechat.com
[6]QR code, www.qrcode.com/en/index.html

application has almost no value and can't count as a competitive advantage. To find information about sending packages with *SaschasSlowPackages*, customers must switch between the mobile app, the web site, and other random online locations.

In comparison, the fictional competitor *DirksFlyingParcels*, which is more or less a clone of *SaschasSlowPackages*, provides a feature-rich mobile application. This application has all kinds of features: tracking packages, showing store locations, calculating shipping prices in different currencies and with different options, integrating with Google Home (*When will my DirksFlyingParcels package arrive in Vancouver?*), chat-based communication with the parcel's sender, and feedback systems.

Most customers will choose *DirksFlyingParcels* simply because the non-functional features are much better covered.

Businesses are very much aware of this. The most prominent example that I am aware of is the Chinese-based app WeChat. My Chinese colleagues tell me, that WeChat has everything they need. They can chat, they can make calls, they can pay, and they can use city services, WeChat even counts steps! There seems to be hardly any need to switch to another app.

Without knowing more details, it is pretty much a given that the system behind WeChat uses (and provides) many API-based integrations. If you look at Figure 3-1 again and concentrate on the lower part, you can see that multiple components are connected to each other. Although it is just a very small example, bigger systems are not much different from an architecture point of view. Each connection represents messages that are being exchanged via APIs.

Modernization

Modernization is a general topic, nothing much to say here. However, businesses are aware that new technologies are born every day and older technologies move into IT heaven. Discussions with customers often go like this: *Sascha, we have this new product and we need to integrate it with our backend systems using APIs. How do we do that and what do we need?* The technology behind "we have this new product" changes over time but "using APIs" is a pattern that has been around for a while and has increasingly become more important.

What I have observed over the last few years is a general increase of products, technologies, and tools that are very much dependent on APIs. The next section on *automatization* will talk about it more, but the complete build process of software products can nowadays be automated using APIs only. Just two or three years ago that wasn't possible, at least not in general!

Due to these trends, businesses have realized that all of the new features must be API driven!

Automatization

In the past, businesses usually did not care too much about the process involved in producing software. They also did not care about processes that were not automated. Needless to say, that those times have changed. With new types of expectations, newer technologies, and faster turn-arounds of product versions, the process of creating software has gained visibility into all layers of executive levels.

Automatization on a large scale cannot be achieved with monolithic systems having proprietary interfaces. To leave those systems behind, businesses now have a new set of terms they want in any software-related project. No matter if it is about building systems or buying products, each piece of enterprise-grade software has to be evaluated against the following criteria:

- **Scalability**: Depending on the current demand, systems need to scale up and down.

- **Upgradability**: Upgrades into production environments with no downtime.

- **Testability**: Whatever code it is, automation has to include tests.

- **Isolation**: Different components should have the least possible dependencies to each other.

- **Configurability**: Configurations for any environment

- **Deployability**: Deployments into any environment

- **Version-ability**: Any system needs to be versioned and rollbacks must be possible.

You may say that none of these terms are especially new in IT. No, they are not. But in the past, each one had manual steps associated with it. Here is an example: until recently I heard the term *white gloves action* often, referring to a *few manual steps* during a software installation or upgrade procedure. Unfortunately, executing these *few* manual steps took up to 12 hours, with no option of rolling back any of them. Luckily, those days are gone or at least they are disappearing. With good automatization coverage, the same process takes about 30 minutes. This is not only an overall shorter timeframe; this also eliminates many potential errors.

Monetization

This is a very important topic, although it does not come up too often during discussions I have. However, businesses are very interested in creating environments that can support APIs for monetization purposes as soon as their systems are ready. In the end, this comes back to the readiness of the omnipresent infrastructure. To monetize APIs, a system needs to be able to audit transactions from an initial request all the way until a response gets returned to the requesting client. Since API-based systems are not directly coupled with each other, they still have to be designed so that values, such as RequestIDs, can be tracked at each step of the way. An example of a business requirement could be this:

Any request needs to be audited and logged in a way so that invoices can be created based on API usage per client and per user.

This requirement may sound simple, but if you look at the small example in Figure 3-1, you can see that it has a big impact on all system components. All APIs have to accept the input and output values included within any request. This has to be considered right from the beginning.

Without an explicit monetization model, APIs are indirectly monetized through products that provide access to audiences that weren't available without the APIs.

Technical Value of APIs

First of all, *APIs are the foundation for realizing business requirements*, especially the ones listed above. This is a very high-level statement, but it is important to be conscious about it (please close your eyes and say it to yourself, very slowly!). Once that becomes the mindset, nobody will be scared of new requirements! The answer will be *We do not have an API for that, but, we can build one!*

I have been in many discussions that interpreted missing APIs as broken products rather than requirements that had not been requested yet. In the right environment, new APIs can be published in a fast, reliable, scalable, well-documented, and well-tested way to support business value within a short period of time.

For some readers, the technical value of APIs may be very obvious, specifically for those who have experience with API-based systems. But for readers who tackle this topic the first time, it may be difficult to see the light at the end of the tunnel. I will try my best to nail it down.

Here is something to remember:

APIs are contracts!

Yes, they are contracts! Chapter 4 talks more about this, but it is so important that I must mention it frequently. Once the contract is written, there shouldn't be any questions and all involved parties can start working. Just like a contract between a homeowner and construction workers, this contract should define requirements that all parties have to adhere to.

These contracts define sets of rules that dictate how a specified business value can be accessed. These contracts are expressed as human-readable and machine-readable documents. They are implemented as programming language-independent interfaces. Here is an example, which is explained in multiple steps.

The Idea

1. The business owns a database that contains lists of users and the products they have purchased in the past.

2. The business wants to make this data available.

3. The data should be made available to different audiences for different purposes.

The Requirements

1. Enable users to retrieve the list of their purchased products.

2. Enable third-party partners to retrieve anonymized lists of all purchased products.

These are two different requirements for the same dataset. This could be a challenge, but not with APIs!

API 1: The List for Users

Human-readable documentation: To retrieve the list of products, **an authenticated user and an authorized application** are required. The communication has to be encrypted. The used message protocol is based on HTTP and the accepted HTTP method is GET. Lists are only produced for the **authenticated user**. An application needs to provide an oauth access_ token as a credential associated with **the user and the application** itself. The list is returned as a JSON message.

Machine-readable documentation: This type of document (Swagger[7]) cannot be shown in all detail here, but the most important pieces include the following:

```
Request-definition:
------------------------
Method: GET
Scheme: HTTPS
Path: /list/products/users
Header: Authorization: Bearer {access_token}
```

---

[7]Swagger, https://swagger.io

```
Response-definition
------------------------
HTTP status: 200
Header: content-type: application/json

Body:
{
  "data": [{
    "user": "{username}",
    "products": [{
      "product": {
        "name": "computer",
        // the payload would be expressed as JSON structure,
        // this is an example of a possible but shortened response
```

API 2: The List for Third Parties

Human-readable documentation: To retrieve the list of products, **an authorized application** is required. The communication has to be encrypted. The used message protocol is based on HTTP and the accepted HTTP method is GET. Lists are produced **with no user information**. An application needs to provide an oauth access_token as a credential associated with **the application** itself. The list is returned as a JSON message.

Machine-readable documentation: The most important pieces are the following:

```
Request-definition:
------------------------
Method: GET
Scheme: HTTPS
Path: /list/products
Header: Authorization: Bearer {access_token}

Response-definition
------------------------
HTTP status: 200
Header: content-type: application/json

Body:
{
  "data": [{
    "user": "",
    "products": [{
      "product": {
        "name": "computer",
        // the payload would be expressed as JSON structure,
        // this is an example of a possible but shortened response
```

Judged by the documentation, the differences are very small. Judged by the responses, the differences are huge! Whereas API I may return a list of tens of values for just one user (see the "user" in the response body), API 2 may produce hundreds of values without user context.

From an API point of view, it comes down to differences only in the Path component of the machine-readable documentation: /list/products/ users vs. /lists/products. In this example, two APIs have to be maintained to support two requirements.

However, in a real-life scenario these APIs could be merged. This is due to the fact that one requirement stated *access_token associated with user and application* and the other stated *access_token associated with application*. This means that API implementations are able to distinguish between access_token associated with users and access_token associated with applications only. This reduces the number of required APIs by 50%. And with that, maintenance, testing, documentation, and scaling tasks are also reduced by 50%.

The documentation could be changed to the following.

API: The List of Products

Human-readable documentation: To retrieve the list of products, an **oauth access_token** is required. The communication has to be encrypted. The used message protocol is based on HTTP and the accepted HTTP method is GET. Lists are produced **without user context** unless the given **oauth access_token** is associated with an **authenticated user**. The list is returned as a JSON message, either with or without user information.

Machine-readable documentation: This document looks as before, except that two different responses are specified:

```
Request-definition:
------------------------
...
Path: /list/products
...
Response-definition: with user context
----------------------------------------------------
...
Body:
{"data": [{"user": "{username}","products": [{ ...
Response-definition: without user context
---------------------------------------------------------
...
Body:
{"data": [{"user": "","products": [{ ...
```

The above documentation has left just one question open: *What happens in error cases?* They would have to be documented as additional responses. In our example, only two errors are possible:

1. **A missing or invalid access_token**: The response would include HTTP status code 401 (unauthorized) and a message containing invalid_request.

2. **Unsupported http method**: The response would include HTTP status code 405 (method not allowed).

The few listed documents specify how these APIs can be consumed and what kind of responses they produce. No questions to be asked. On the other hand, none of the documents have named any details about the API implementation itself. And that is the beauty! No consumer of those APIs needs to know! Not needing to know has advantages:

- Foremost, the API consumer can be any type of application, independent of the programming language.

- Any HTTP-capable testing tool can be used. No specific programming language is required.

Let's have a look at Figure 3-2, derived from Figure 3-1. If all the components depend on programming language-specific interfaces, it would almost be impossible to keep the system running.

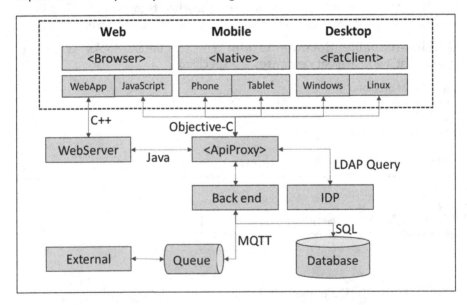

Figure 3-2. *Components providing interfaces of different programming languages*

Communications via APIs, on the other hand, have no notion of language whatsoever. Components can be replaced, and implementations can be updated. As long as the APIs stay the same, there is not even a need to share the information about updated or replaced components.

Another topic is **testing**!

The API is well defined, and all types of requests and responses are documented. Testing tools that are capable of processing machine readable documents can generate code stubs. These code stubs can be completed, and automated tests can be executed. Due to the nature of APIs not exposing or documenting implementation details, they can be tested using a **black box**[8] approach. This reduces the number of required test cases and eliminates the need for manual tests. Except for sanity checks, APIs do not need a lot *of personal love!*

After looking at this example and listing a few advantages of using APIs, I would like to circle back and look at some of the general business requirements and how they can be satisfied with APIs. I am listing them in order of their importance and how customers usually prioritize them.

- **Integrations**: This is the top reason for using APIs. I have not seen any other topic named as often as this one. Enterprise systems are fully stacked with all kinds of products. All of these products were acquired from different vendors that use different technologies and were not designed to work hand-in-hand with other products. Needless to say, customers still want those products to work together and exchange messages using one way or the other.

  The only common feature practically all products share is the ability to consume and provide APIs. With that, integrations are possible and actively used. Of course, it is not always as straightforward as it may sound. There are cases where products are flexible enough to be modified, so that required APIs can be made available. But sometimes that is not possible. In those scenarios *ApiProxys* come into play. They are made to be adjusted to any API and take on the role of a mediator. They receive messages on one API, translate it to another, and forward the message to the recipient.

  Either way, with or without ApiProxy, APIs enable integrations and with that business requirements can be satisfied

---

[8]Black box testing, http://softwaretestingfundamentals.com/black-box-testing/

- **Upgradability/deployability**: Upgrading and deploying software components are very different tasks. However, from an API point of view these two tasks are very similar. Customers usually do not specifically require APIs as such in this context, but they require command-line interfaces (CLIs). CLIs are used for integrations with build tools and to eliminate the need for manual actions. Even in this case APIs are the enabler. The exciting part is that those APIs can support command-line interfaces but also UI-driven tools. One API, multiple use cases supported!

- **Configurability**: Configuration files are persisted and managed using version control systems such as *Git*.[9] In conjunction with online services such as *GitHub*,[10] these files can be managed via APIs. Having the APIs available, it can be imagined how these APIs can be used to move configurations onto a software component.

- **Testability**: I have spoken to developers who work in a fully automated environment. They finish their implementation, including tests, and submit the code to the version control system. Once that is done, they do not even known when and how their code moves into the production environment. They will only hear back if a test has failed during the automated deployment process.

- **Version-ability**: This does not only reference the ability of defining version numbers after a configuration has been applied to a software component. No, this also refers to the idea of activating and deactivating different components without manual intervention. A typical use is the selection of a specific deployment by version. Workflows can be supported this way, such as *deploy version 1.2.00, test it and tag it, if successfully tested, but remove it and redeploy the previous version if the test fails.* This is another use case where APIs are the enabler!

I hope this section helps you understand the importance and relevance of APIs from a technical point of view. I encourage you to take some time and experiment with APIs using existing tools and platforms. After a few successful tests, the whole picture will come together nicely. I can almost promise that!

---

[9]Git, https://git-scm.com
[10]GitHub, https://github.com/features

Business Requirements vs. Technical Requirements

Most (verbal) fights that I have witnessed during my IT career were fought between members of business and engineering teams. Product owners and architects want a slick and easy-to-use application. These applications should also be safe to use, reliable, maintainable, modularized, future proof, scalable, modern, well architected, documented, and tested. Generally, product owners and architects are on the same page. But for some reason, product owners will sometimes say something along these lines, which emphasizes their different views:

We have a release date and we need to get something out of the door. Please come up with an MVP (minimum viable product) that I can take to my boss!

My personal reaction is this: *Really? How is the proposed product not an MVP already? And why do we still talk about release dates in a CI/CD[11]-driven world?*

I have been on the engineering side of things always, but I still have a hard time following the release date arguments. As someone with a background in machinery and who has repaired helicopters, my feeling is that the software business is far from being comparable with other industries. Can you imagine the following discussion in aeronautics?

> *We have scheduled the first public flight with passengers of SpacePlane-X75 for September. The engines won't be fully tested by then and cannot be started if the outside temperature is below 25 degrees Celsius. However, we cannot move the date. Please come up with an MVP that I can take to my boss.*

> *OK, I got it, here it is: preheat the engines and do not run them with more than 80% of their capacity. That should take us off the ground and three months later we will fly again to show off what we can really do!*

I would now like to share some cases of "business vs. engineering" discussions that I have witnessed. Some of them may sound familiar; some may even be based on talks between you and me. Please do not be confused by technical terms you may not know; it is more about the type of conversation. My recommendations are stated in the row named Recommendation. You may want to consider it too.

- **Topic: Authentication** = No redirect wanted

    Business: We want to use the authorization_code flow but do not want users to be redirected to a different location.

---

[11]CI/CD, Continuous integration/continuous delivery

Engineer: It is essential to redirect to the third-party server to highlight to users that they are not sharing their third-party credentials with our system.

Business: Redirects scare users and give us bad ratings in the app store.

Conclusion: An iFrame will be displayed on the current web site that contains the third-party server login page. Unfortunately, this will leave users skeptical since they cannot identify the owner of the login screen. Critical users will not consider using your application in the future.

Recommendation: Redirect users to the third-party server. Users need to see the security-icon and who's hosting the login page in the browser URL. This addresses privacy concerns.

- **Topic: Authorization** = No explicit consent wanted

Business: We do not want users to see a consent page.

Engineer: Third-party applications need an explicit consent by our users before sharing personal details.

Business: Most users are not aware of that anyways and the consent screen will distract them. This will give us bad ratings in the app stores.

Conclusion: Authorization flows will be modified to skip the consent screen; third-party apps will be configured as preauthorized.

Recommendation: Display the consent screen at least once! Whenever you empower users, they feel respected and in charge of their own data, leading them to trust us more.

- **Topic: Session** = Never-ending session wanted

Business: We do not want users to log in more than once until they actively logout.

Engineer: We cannot trust any type of token-based credential with an endless lifetime if no proof-of-possession is supported.

Business: You know what we want. Find a solution.

Conclusion: Authorization servers will be configured to issue a session token that has an endless
lifetime. Leaking tokens enable unauthorized entities
(either applications or persons or both) to imperson-
ate users. If users ever discover this, they will abandon
this company.

Recommendation: Issue a short-lived token to
consume resources and a long-lived token to retrieve
a new short-lived token. Exchange the long-lived token
only via backchannel communication. Implement a
flow that proves that users still own the session but
avoid any knowledge-based techniques (most famous
one: **What is your mother's maiden name?).**
Instead, have users prove the ownership of devices.
For anything users feel is important to them (like bank
accounts) they will not mind having to prove that they
are the eligible owner of almost anything.

These three example discussions come up over and over again. Usually it is
the business side that wants engineers to find solutions that enable custom
message flows, for example, in OAuth 2.0. When I get involved, I do not
feel that I am answering technical questions. I mean, the questions I get are
always based on technology. But they reflect requirements that were stated
by businesses, and with that, an implementation change is not a change in
technology but an enablement for the business.

In the beginning, I interpreted these types of changes/requirements as a kind
of disconnect between businesses and their engineers. But over the last few
years I have realized that I am wrong. Although there will always be conflicts,
especially when required modifications raise privacy or security concerns, in
the end, technology is not available for the sake of technology but to make
businesses happen. And what I have learned from that is this:

APIs are the foundation for realizing business requirements!

Summary

It is important for any involved party to know why APIs are relevant in their
specific case. Without knowing this, wrong decisions will be made, and the
success of any API project will be in jeopardy. The overall business goals of
reducing costs and gaining revenue will not be achieved. If this chapter was a
success, it should be easier to follow arguments toward systems that are fully
API-driven.

API Design

Although there are many types of APIs for many different purposes, there are common aspects that should be considered independently of the use case. After reading this chapter, a foundational knowledge should be available.

General Guidelines

After becoming a member of Twitter, one of my very first tweets was the following:

> When designing APIs, it will either be simple or complicated. There is little in between #APIManagement

That was in February, 2015. By the time this book is published, that statement will be three and a half years old. I have been working with APIs almost every day since then and I think that statement is still valid!

I wrote that statement after getting the task of designing a storage API. These were the requirements, functional and more or less non-functional:

- Functional:
  - A client sends a request including a message to be persisted. The API returns a key associated with the persisted message.
  - A client sends a request to retrieve the persisted message. The client includes the issued key that identifies the message.

© CA 2018

S. Preibisch, *API Development*, https://doi.org/10.1007/978-1-4842-4140-0_4

- Non-Functional:
    - Only the client is able to retrieve the message.

So far, so good. Sounds simple, right?

If you ever get a "simple" requirement like this, you have to ask questions! Otherwise, you may assume what the intended behavior should be. Do not mistake unanswered questions or undefined behavior as implementation details! For example, if you order a car, you will most likely include the desired color. If you do not, the car manufacturer will ask you for that information. He will not assume which color you want!

Here is a list of questions based on those requirements:

- Are there limitations in regard to the message size?
- Are there limitations in regard to the number of messages a single client can persist?
- Are messages persisted forever or is there an expiration time?
- Are there requirements in regard to the issued key?
- Should messages be encrypted when not in use and stored in the database (encrypted at rest)?
- Should a client be able to request a list of all keys that have been issued to it?
- Should a client be able to replace or update an existing message?
- How should a client authenticate itself?

This example started off simple but became very complicated very quickly. However, asking all these questions early will save a lot of resources in the long run!

The questions above are very specific to that one API. But there are general questions about APIs. A few are below. They are the typical ones I receive in my current role from customers:

- Shall we use SSL or SSL with client authentication?
- Shall we accept certificates signed by well-known certificate authorities (CA) or act as a CA and sign CSRs[1]?
- Shall we check for message sizes?
- Shall we include a rate limit check?
- How shall we authenticate the requesting user?

---

[1]CSR, certificate signing request

In general, the types of questions have not changed over the last few years. Anybody who wants to expose APIs is simply concerned about the security, accessibility, usability, reliability, and general protection of their systems.

However, more often questions around OAuth, OpenID Connect, JSON Web Token, and microservices come up these days. When these questions are asked, it is not uncommon to see them in combination with the desire of wanting to adhere to an RFC but also to add customizations. In addition, the questions are often combined with a conversation that starts like this: *Sascha, our case is very special, and it is really complicated.* In most cases, it actually turns out to be complicated but not unique! I have observed this especially in cases where different authentication and authorization schemes need to be combined. Many customers have to support legacy systems that need to be used in conjunction with newer methods. Getting their head around useful and secure combinations is not often required and therefore new to most developers I work with. I sometimes compare the perception of the asking customer with a situation where something was new to me.

For example, some time ago I bought a motorhome. As soon as I got it, the following happened: I found videos on the topic of motorhomes, I found motorhome sections in supermarkets, and I found specialized shops in my area. I never noticed those supermarket sections and shops before. After talking to me, developers often realize that their situation wasn't as unique as they thought and not as complicated as they anticipated.

Usually I get involved very late in the design process of a solution after developers already went too far down the wrong path to completely fix it in a given timeframe. (*You may have heard of the timeframe: It is too late, we are going live next week.*) In those cases, a rescue mission gets reduced to minimal changes that improve the system behavior but primarily identify potential enhancements for the next release. These are frustrating situations considering the fact that an initial design meeting (or a few) could have changed the complete path of execution.

It is very important for any future system to discuss the design with someone who asks questions, provides constructive criticism, has a high-level understanding of the targeted solution, and whose goal it is not to entertain his ego. As a matter of fact, it is about defending the design against others. If that is successful, the chances for having a good design are high.

Without getting very detailed, there are a few guidelines that should always be considered as part of any API design session:

- **Good documentation:** This is the first step towards API adoption. Always look at it this way: anything that is not documented does not exist! If you want features to be adopted, make them visible to your target audience. In addition to human-readable documentation, provide documents such as Swagger.[2] This enables developers to use your API with less manual programming effort. Some libraries will even generate code stubs based on Swagger documents. I know that some will say, *Good code does not need documentation.* That may be (partially) true for programming languages but not for APIs. If a developer browses a catalog of APIs with no explanation of what they do and how they behave, it will become a matter of trial and error. And since good APIs will expose limited information about errors only, it is nearly impossible for developers to figure out how particular APIs may be used.

- **Standards-based interfaces:** In most cases, a RESTful interface is widely accepted as good practice and well understood by developers. Do not try to be creative; use that creativity somewhere else.

- **Performance:** As a professor during my studies used to say, *The only thing that matters is performance, performance, performance!* And I agree; it is very important. Unfortunately, it is difficult to measure. It depends on the use case. You must define data points yourself. Performance data points should be specified as part of the general SLA[3] of your API. When specifying the SLA, include response times, numbers of supported requests per time frame, maximum number of concurrent requests, maximum message sizes, and anything a developer needs to know when consuming your APIs. Without an SLA, you are opening the door for complaints and your only (helpless) answer will be *Let me check; I have no idea!*

- **Versioning:** Your API should be versioned. Do not break interfaces from one release to another.

On the same note, make sure you pay attention to challenges that are especially known for HTTP-based API systems:

- **Statelessness:** HTTP APIs are stateless by design. Extra effort is required to support state.

- **Latency:** The time a request travels from a client computer to the server computer that implements the API. The overall latency includes server-side processing time too. Practically each hop in a network adds latency! We had customers who have said, *I do not want latency!*

---

[2]Swagger, https://swagger.io
[3]SLA, service-level agreement

If your product cannot reduce latency, we will not consider it!
Latency cannot be removed, so be aware of the fact and
introduce a test system that identifies latency between
different hops. You need to isolate the bottlenecks that
add latency; otherwise you will try changing your system
in the wrong areas, which I have seen often.

- **Reliability:** You need to specify the required availability.
  Having APIs available for 100% of the time is a big effort.
  This topic requires serious discussions during the design
  phase. For example, in this moment while I am writing, my
  blogging platform service provider has closed the system
  for a period of 12 hours! If you are a bank or a gaming
  platform, you may want to choose a design that requires
  none or very short maintenance windows.

- **Accessibility:** Once an API is available, there must be
  rules regarding its accessibility. Who can consume it when
  and how often? On one hand, this is a technical question
  but from a product owners' perspective you may want to
  clarify who the intended audience should be.

If you start your working sessions with a checklist that contains the topics
above, you have done the first step towards a good API!

Getting Started

In a new project, it is always difficult to get from nothing to something that
is working and can be used for further detailing. To get off the ground, I
always recommend starting with a design document, taking the "contract first"
approach. You must create a design document that is machine readable. Some
developers say this is too hard, but in my point of view there is nothing better
than it.

Here is an example of how to get documentation, working test clients, working
test suites, mock service stubs, all of that with just a few clicks. I use open
source tools that help me regularly; they may help you, too. Try the following
to get an idea of the flow:

1. Open a Swagger example document at *editor.swagger.io*.
   The content will be similar to Figure 4-1. Use it as your
   starting point. It may take some time to get used to it, but
   once you get the hang of it, it should become the default
   approach. The document contains a basic description, the

host name (line 14), supported schemes (lines 16, 17), the URL path (line 23), and the response (line 27). The document can be copied onto your machine as JSON[4] or YAML[5] file.

```
1    swagger: '2.0'
2    info:
3      version: 1.0.0
4      title: Basic Auth Example
5      description: >
6        An example for how to use Basic Auth with Swagger.
7        Server code is available [here](https://github.com/mohsen1/basic-auth-server).
8        It's running on Heroku.
9
10       **User Name and Password**
11       * User Name: `user`
12       * Password: `pass`
13
14   host: basic-auth-server.herokuapp.com
15   schemes:
16     - http
17     - https
18   securityDefinitions:
19     basicAuth:
20       type: basic
21       description: HTTP Basic Authentication. Works over `HTTP` and `HTTPS`
22   paths:
23     /:
24       get:|
25         security:
26           - basicAuth: []
27         responses:
28           '200':
29             description: Will send `Authenticated` if authentication is succesful,
30               otherwise it will send `Unauthorized`
```

Figure 4-1. *Example Swagger API definition*

2. While you are developing the Swagger document, the same screen will generate a UI. This UI contains two parts: one static component and one dynamic component that lets you execute your APIs. Figures 4-2 and 4-3 show these screens.

---

[4]JSON, www.w3schools.com/js/js_json_intro.asp
[5]YAML, http://yaml.org

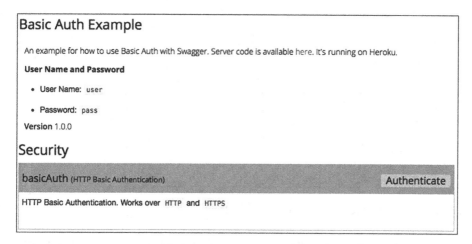

Figure 4-2. Static view

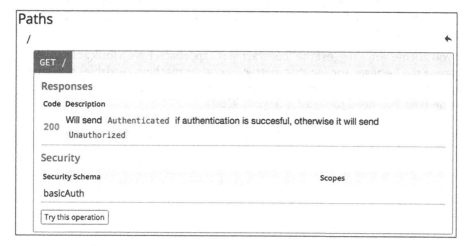

Figure 4-3. Dynamic view. The "Try this operation" button actually works!

3. Once you are happy with your API document, the next tool waits for you. It is SOAPUI[6] (which is my personal preference, but other tools can certainly be used). SOAPUI can import the Swagger file to get started with your testing effort. Figure 4-4 shows a screenshot. You can find a generated test request (Request 1), a TestSuite (TestSuite 1) with a test case, and a section of load tests (Load Tests). In addition, a mock service was generated (REST MockService 1).

---

[6]SOAPUI, www.soapui.org

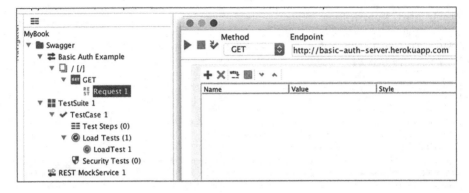

Figure 4-4. SOAPUI, after importing a swagger document

With very little effort you can now start playing around with your API, you can find issues in your design, and you can discuss your findings with other team members. Although I have not mentioned how to design APIs yet, at least you now have tools at hand to help you put the bits and pieces together once you get there.

If you ask me why I suggest the "contract first" approach, have a look at Figure 4-5. Having the Swagger (or for that matter, any other machine-readable) document available, team members can start working on their part of the project at the same time. No need to wait for anyone else!

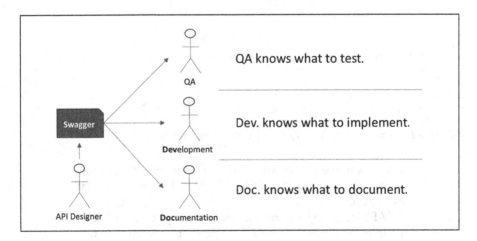

Figure 4-5. Team members can begin working at the same time. The role of the API Designer is usually taken on by a developer together with a product owner.

Another advantage is that all details of the API have to be specified explicitly. In comparison, if you take a code *first and generate a Swagger* approach you totally depend on that "generation tool" doing the right thing. That is bad since *you* need to be in control of your API and not some random tool! In addition, modifications of the API are most likely required between the "first shot" and the final result. This is easy to handle if the "contract" gets updated and all other artifacts follow the changes. Otherwise, the implementation may be updated, but not exposed in the contract. And with that, all other dependent groups will miss out and fail at some point in time.

Designing the First API

The difference between *using APIs* and *designing APIs* is not too obvious. It is like *eating a meal* and *preparing a meal*! After having eaten many meals, it may seem easy to prepare one. However, once you are on the other side of the kitchen counter, it is pretty different!

The same applies to APIs. If you have used one, it may feel easy to design one yourself. Nevertheless, using an API, implementing an API, and designing an API are not comparable tasks. Further down, it is all about designing APIs.

The following sections contain a few tips that always work.

Choose the Right Name for the API

Imagine that a developer browses through a registry of APIs. He is looking for easy and clear names that indicate what the API does. Some examples are *Manage User Attributes* if the API manages user attributes and *List User Attributes* if the API is a read-only API.

Choose an HTTP Method

It is very common to use them like this:

- GET: Retrieve data
- POST: Submit data
- PUT/PATCH: Update data
- DELETE: Delete data

Sometimes GET and POST are both accepted. If you attempt to do so, document GET to be used with query parameters and POST with a message body.

Before I move on, there are a few rules an API should adhere to. All HTTP methods have expected responses by convention. This is crucial, please pay attention.

- GET: A response should have HTTP status 200.

  - Implementing an API that does so will comply with libraries that are commonly used.

- DELETE: A response should have HTTP status 200 or 204

  - Status 200 indicates a successful request with a payload in the response.

  - Status 204 indicates a successful response but with no payload whatsoever.

- POST, PUT: A response should have HTTP status 200.

  - If POST created a message, provide the created message in the response, even if it is a copy! If the POST request message got enriched with added values such as a creation date, it is even more important.

  - If PUT modified a message, return the final result!

Enabling clients to use the smallest number of requests to fulfill a task is a best practice.

Choose the scheme, such as HTTP or HTTPS

Using HTTP should be an exception, HTTPS is the way to go. If you ever hear an argument against HTTPS due to costly SSL (TLS) certificates, you can easily put an end to that discussion. The certificate authority Let's Encrypt[7] is free of charge and its signed certificates are accepted by all browsers and practically all libraries.

On the other hand, even when using HTTPS, it is not always necessary to have publicly signed certificates. If your system provides the server and the client, those two entities can be built to trust self-signed certificates.

Choose the right URL Path

This is a tough one. There is no single right answer. URL paths (sometimes also called "routes") have to be considered together with the HTTP method. Here are examples:

- Retrieving a single attribute of a single user:

  - GET /manage/user/{userId}/attribute/{attrId}

    - {userId} would be substituted by a user Id

---

[7]Let's Encrypt, https://letsencrypt.org

- {attrId} would be substituted by an attribute Id
- The response would include exactly one attribute of exactly one user.

- Submit attributes for a single user:

  - POST /manage/user/{userId}

    - {"attributes": [{"age":66}]} ← payload
    - Requests that submit data should carry the data (payload) within the body of the request.
    - The HTTP header Content-Type has to be provided. In this case, since JSON gets submitted, the value would be application/json.

- Updating attributes for a single user:

  - PUT /manage/user/{userId}

    - {"attributes": [{"age":67}]}
    - More or less a copy of the POST request, but PUT indicates that existing attributes are updated

- Deleting an attribute of a user:

  - DELETE /manage/user/{userId}/attribute/{attrId}

Do not build APIs that ignore the HTTP method but instead require the task in the URL path (.../user/get?userId={userId}) instead of GET .../user/{userId})! I have done that in the past and it causes confusion.

Specify useful response messages

All tips are important, but this one has potential to make a difference like day and night. Whatever you do, always keep the following in mind:

APIs are meant for machines, not people!

This is so important because response messages that are meant for people are not usable in a machine-to-machine environment! This may seem obvious, but it is not to everyone. When machines communicate with each other, they should be able to *go with the flow*. By that I mean, a request message should result in a response message that completes a task but should not require further requests. Here are two bad examples. I was responsible for the first one myself.

1. An API persists a message. The response is `true`.

2. An API deploys a new service API. The response is

    `{"success": "the API has been deployed successfully"}`.

Both responses may be useful for a person, but not for a machine. Here is why:

1. The persisted message was enhanced with data such as an ID, a creation date, and a status. But the submitting entity never knew about that!

2. The deployed service was enhanced with an ID. That ID was the only way to retrieve details about this service. Unfortunately, the requestor never got the value! The really bad part about this was that there was potential for a timely gap between "deployed" and "active." A requestor had to poll the API to find out if the service became active. That poll required the ID! The requestor now had to send another API request to get a list of deployed services, find his by searching for it by name, and then extract the ID.

    To illustrate this even further, look at Figure 4-6. It has a section for a *bad response*. To find out if the newly deployed service is active, a client needs to send further requests to get the needed information about the deployment *status*. This could have been completely avoided by responding with *all details* right way!

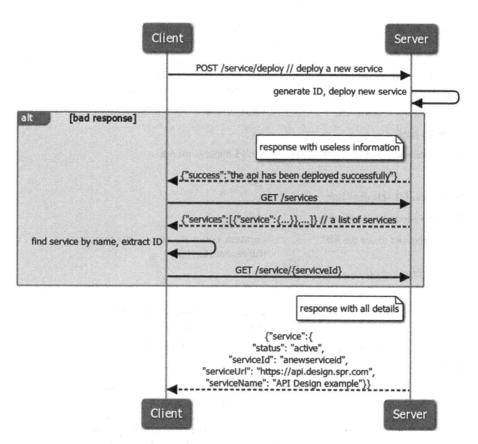

Figure 4-6. Bad response vs. good response

When I used the deploy API the first time, I got angry! I believe other users got angry, too. API design should avoid those mistakes whenever possible!

Table 4-1 is very simple but it covers high-level information about an API. It can be used as a starting point for discussions.

Table 4-1. High-level Information About an API

General Info	
What is the purpose of the API?	This API receives a location and returns information about the current weather.
What is the name of the API?	Weather info
Is this API public ?	Yes
Are maintenance windows acceptable?	Yes, 15 minutes/month

High-Level, Technical Info	
Do clients need to authenticate?	No
What is required to use the API?	Location, optional a unit for the temperature (Fahrenheit, Celsius)
Which HTTP methods (verbs) are supported?	GET
What is included in a response?	Location with city, province, country, temperature, unit, a weather icon
What is the response message type?	JSON (JavaScript Object Notation)
Example of a success response	``` { "weather": [{"city": "Vancouver", "province": "British Columbia (BC)", "country": "Canada", "temperature": "21", "unit": "Celsius", "icon": "https://url.to.an.image"}] } ```
Example of an error response	``` { "error": "invalid_request", "error_description":"the given location is unknown" } ```

When this table is passed around to team members, questions will arise. About 60% of questions and complaints can be addressed even before anyone starts working on it in any way.

Going a Little Further

Usually APIs are part of a larger ecosystem. A single API by itself will often not be very useful. When APIs are built, each one takes on a small role among others. This is already the case within a small web site. Each button on a web site will send a request to an API, in many cases a specific API just for this button. For example, a menu item on a web site may be labeled *About*. If the menu gets selected, there may be entries such as *Contact, Who we are, Office locations,* and *Legal.* This may result in four APIs!

Continuing this example, each single API has to be designed for itself, but also in conjunction with the others. A web site has no flow; buttons or menu items are selected randomly. Therefore, when designing APIs that are meant to work together as one application, they must accommodate all cases; either selected in an expected or random order. Table 4-1 is a good example. Let me emphasize the *WebApp* and *WebServer* components in the derived Figure 4-7.

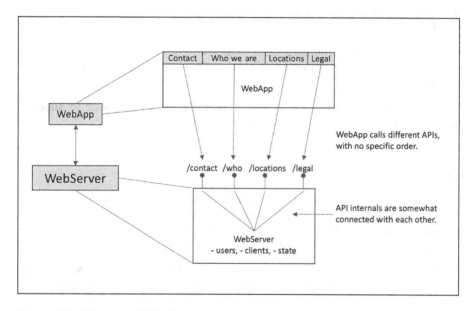

Figure 4-7. WebApp and WebServer manage multiple APIs

The web application (WebApp) has no way of controlling the flow in which the APIs, hosted on the web server (WebServer), are being called. The challenge is that the APIs should not have hard dependencies to each other. On the other hand, the web server may need to handle state across those APIs.

In the end, it becomes a challenge within the API implementation, not so much in the design of the API. Nevertheless, those *soft dependencies* have to be considered. In Chapter 6, which covers implementation details, examples will be covered. When discussing microservices in Chapter 8, this topic will be relevant again.

User Interface vs. BackEnd API Design

User interface-driven API design approaches the topic with a focus on serving user interfaces (UIs).

Backend–driven API design approaches the topic with a focus on serving backend systems.

I am not sure if this is a typical differentiator, but at least I like to do it this way. It allows me to start the design process with completely different mind sets, matching the requirement. Another way to emphasize the difference is by use case for each type of API.

A use case for UI-driven API design: *UIs need data structures that contain everything they require to fill up UI elements with data after just one request and one response (ideally)!*

A use case for backend–driven API design: *Backend APIs need to support command-line tools that integrate with operational systems!*

UI-Driven API Design

The idea behind it is simple. For example, an online banking web application has a *View Accounts* button. After clicking it, the UI displays the most important account details. Immediately! This behavior is not possible if the UI does not receive what it needs in its preferred format.

To get a better understanding, recall Figure 4-6. Imagine the *bad response* in this scenario, even extended to multiple bad ones, as shown in Figure 4-8.

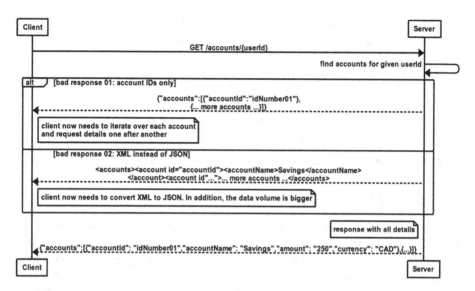

Figure 4-8. Bad responses

Bad Response 01 includes account IDs only, which is pretty much useless for the client. The client has to iterate over the list of account IDs and send one request each to the server to retrieve details for the matching account. For users with one account, that may be acceptable, but otherwise the usability of this web application is dreadful.

Bad Response 02 returns all required details but in the wrong message format. The client now needs to transform the message first so that details can be selected and displayed.

UI-driven APIs have several requirements that are especially relevant. Before I list them, please remember: always assume that a web application is used from a mobile device, which has a data plan and should only be stressed for good reasons!

- **Data volume**: The required data volume should be reduced to a minimum. One response with a large message may be better than multiple medium-sized ones.

- **Network traffic**: Fewer required requests to run an application are better. If an application needs to execute requests every other moment, it will fail sooner or later, especially on mobile devices that have limited network connectivity. It will also impact the server due to constant, unnecessary requests.

- **Message types:** Always remember, UI developers are very lazy! They want data served in a format that can be used as is with little effort. This is not meant as criticism; they just know what they need. What they do not need are messages that need a lot of massaging before they can be processed. Implementing a user-friendly UI is already a big challenge by itself. Always consult UI developers in UI-driven API projects!

Long story short, enable UI developers as much as possible!

BackEnd–Driven API Design

In many cases, APIs are consumed by command-line tools (clients) such as curl[8]. They can be optimized for very different purposes. Handling XML or CSV files, handling data connections, orchestrating APIs, aggregating different messages, and requiring and returning minimal data are some of their tasks and requirements. Backend–driven APIs are often designed to integrate with command-line tools. Nowadays, where CI/CD processes are becoming more important, command-line tools depend on APIs that are meant for configuration updates, build execution, or deployments of software.

Contrary to UI-driven APIs, these APIs should return only the minimum information that is needed. In addition, responses should return values that can be piped into other commands. I would not call myself a command-line wizard, but here is an example.

When working with Docker[9], a command-line tool allows you to start, stop and remove docker containers. They are not REST APIs, but they demonstrate how a good interface may be designed.

- Run *tomcat* version 8, map port 80 to port 8080, name the container *mytomcat*, stop the container, and remove it.

    - `docker run -p 80:8080 --name mytomcat tomcat:8`

    - `docker stop mytomcat`

    - `docker rm mytomcat`

- Stop and remove all running docker containers.

    - `docker stop $(docker ps -aq) && docker rm $(docker ps -aq)`

---

[8]curl, `https://curl.haxx.se/docs/httpscripting.html`
[9]Docker, `www.docker.com/what-docker`

The command $(docker ps -aq) returns just the numeric IDs of available containers, which are passed to docker stop and docker rm. No need to know IDs explicitly! Having those commands available makes it easy to integrate with a CI/CD tool chain. UI-based clients would most likely need to have an indicator such as id=idnumberone&id=idnumbertwo.

Combining Both Types of APIs

Many projects do not start off without an inventory of APIs. The cases I have seen were mainly backend API heavy. The questions I often receive are on the topic of connecting UIs to existing backend APIs.

The first thought that may come to mind is to use the existing APIs as they are and have the client transform or enrich data to serve a UI. As you have just seen, APIs that were not made for serving UIs will reduce the functionality, which will reduce the acceptance of the application by users and the project will suffer.

Instead, it is good practice to implement an abstraction layer in-between the UI and the backend API. Figure 3-1 already gave a hint on how to approach this challenge. A component called *API Proxy* was introduced. An API Proxy takes on the task of translating UI-driven needs to backend APIs and vice versa.

A typical case could look like Figure 4-9. A backend provides APIs that return very specific data only. For example, one API returns user profiles, another an email address, one home addresses, and one phone numbers of a user. If a UI wants to display a single page with all of those values, it would have to send a request to each of them. Instead, the API Proxy provides a single API called /userinfo that aggregates the data.

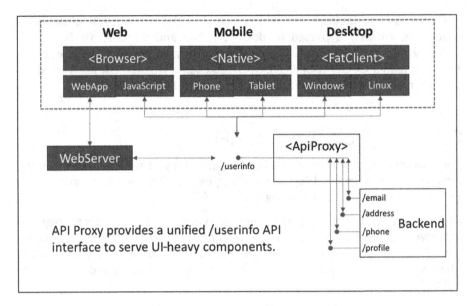

Figure 4-9. API Proxy provides a unified API interface

As discussed earlier, API Proxy can also provide an API per type of client. Using that approach enables systems to leverage existing backend APIs and expose them to needs of any type of client.

Summary

Investing time and resources into the early stages of API design will create efficient and reliable systems. APIs that are not optimized for specific use cases are just as costly as a weak foundation when building a house. It may look promising in the beginning, but it will take down the whole system sooner or later. The guidelines provided in this chapter should give you a good idea of the topics that need to be considered to get good APIs.

API Authentication and Authorization

After discussing API design patterns, I would like to dedicate a complete chapter to this topic due to its importance. All APIs need to know who they are being used by. The answer is provided via authentication and authorization mechanisms. Whatever gets implemented, always remember this:

Authentication and authorization keep data private and shared between authorized entities only!

Authentication vs. Authorization

In any system, almost all relevant APIs require users, or at least clients, to authenticate. And at some point in time, an API will require authorizations, too. It is very important to consider this fact in the first design sessions. The whole API project will be very different without these two attributes.

There are two important questions you must ask. The first question is *What is the difference between authentication and authorization?* The answer is quite simple:

© CA 2018
S. Preibisch, *API Development*, https://doi.org/10.1007/978-1-4842-4140-0_5

Authentication answers who I am whereas authorization answers what I can do!

In this statement, "I" could be a user (a person) or a client (an application). I hope that you agree. That's all there is to say about it.

The second question is *What should happen when during message flows?* The answer to this question is very different and more complex. The (hopefully) obvious part of the answer is the following:

Only authenticated entities can be authorized!

If an entity is unknown, it is not possible to authorize access to any resources for it. This means whatever flow is executed, authentication happens first!

To get things right, potential authentication methods should be discussed early in the design process. Whatever is chosen influences API interfaces, the API implementation, the infrastructure of the environment, potentially the overall performance, and privacy statements. Here are a few methods as a first overview:

- Username and password as parameters
- HTTP basic authentication
- x.509 certificates
- HTTP cookies
- SAML
- JWT
- Other token-based systems

The chosen option needs to be respected in the API interface design. It makes a difference if HTTP basic authentication is required rather than, let's say, username and password as parameters. The API definitions would include the following:

Case: HTTP basic authentication

- HTTP methods: GET, POST, PUT, DELETE, PATCH, and more
- HTTP header: `Authorization: Basic bXk6Ym9vaw==`
- Content-Type: Any

Case: Username, password as parameters

- HTTP methods: POST, PUT, PATCH, and more. However, the payload (message body) needs to include username, password. If that is not possible in your use case, this method is not an option!

- Content-Type: application/x-www-form-urlencoded. Others are possible, but do not comply with HTTP Form POST mechanisms and require manual extraction of the values on incoming requests.

- Note: Methods like GET or DELETE may include username and password as URL query parameters, but I do not consider them viable options (i.e. GET /authenticate? username=bob&password=secret)

With any method certain advantages and disadvantages will be introduced! In any case, the API uses the incoming credentials and validates them. Most likely that involves an identity provider (IDP). That, again, influences the overall system due to the required type of IDP that has to be made available.

Once the authentication is successful, authorization follows. Here is the most common question on that topic:

Should the authorization decision be made in conjunction with the authentication step or only when it actually is needed?

If that is not clear, here is an example. Many apps on mobile devices need to access certain resources such as contacts. Some apps request authorization for that right after or during the installation. These apps *preemptively request authorization.* Other apps prompt for authorization just in time when they need it.

To make the decision of when to request authorization, use cases have to be considered. But not only! Let me repeat the figure that shows components connected via APIs (Figure 5-1) and discuss a few arguments to think about.

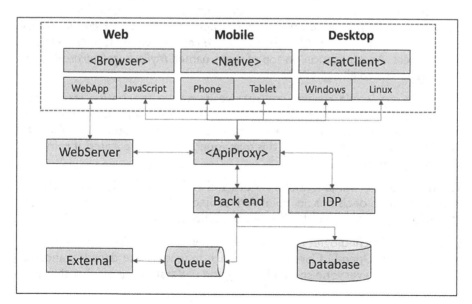

Figure 5-1. Components connected via APIs

Preemptive Authorizations

Let's say a JavaScript app needs access to the database and to the queue via two different APIs. The JavaScript app first has a user authenticated against the IDP and then requests authorizations for those two APIs in the same moment. <ApiProxy> has a mechanism to grant those authorizations and issue a JWT that contains these authorization statements. The JavaScript app now uses that JWT on both APIs exposed on <ApiProxy>. Both APIs validate the JWT, check for a required authorization statement, and grant or deny the request. <ApiProxy> forwards the request to the matching APIs on the backend. **Here's the catch**: Both APIs know that the JavaScript app has other authorizations! That may be acceptable but maybe not! In these situations, always be pessimistic and act in favor of privacy!

It would be better to send a request to those APIs at <ApiProxy> with a credential only. This would be validated and now, at this point in time for this API only, <ApiProxy> would create an authorization statement that is forwarded to the matching API at the backend.

Just-in-Time Authorizations

If you imagine an API-based system that never uses preemptive but just-in-time authorizations only, you can easily imagine that the network traffic would potentially grow by a big number. A lot of noise would decrease the performance for the overall system. Therefore, a compromise between both approaches has to be found.

My recommendation is to grant authorization statements within APIs that serve the same application. For example, the fictional *HandlePackages* application is based on five APIs; the *FindLostParcels* application is built on top of three others. An application on top of them, named *MyPackageAndParcelBuddy*, requires access to all eight APIs.

The single app would request and receive its own authorization statements and would not share them. But *MyPackageAndParcelBuddy* would now need two different ones: one authorization statement for each feature and with that one per group of APIs. Although this may sound more complicated, it removes the privacy issues.

The next section will talk about OAuth and JWT in more detail and should help you make decisions in your API project. OAuth is an authorization framework that helps with both types of authorizations.

Of all available technologies that could be chosen for this task I will concentrate on OAuth and OpenID Connect. These are practically the default standards of our time, and everyone should have a good understanding of what they are.

OAuth

In today's API-based systems OAuth is a technology that is found almost everywhere. I get many questions about OAuth, I wrote many blog posts about this topic, and I have created a web site that has oauth in its name (www.oauth.blog). However, even though this technology has been around for quite some time, it seems to be challenging.

Here is something you may have heard before. And if not, please pay attention:

OAuth is an authorization *framework*!

This is easier said than understood. If it is not clear, here is a list of what OAuth *is not*:

- OAuth is not made for authentication.

- OAuth is not a replacement of known authentication schemes.

- OAuth is not a fixed protocol.

- OAuth is not a list of well-defined features or use cases.

If you are not quite sure yet, do not worry. Here is a question I have read on Twitter that emphasizes that many people have trouble understanding it:

Are you using LDAP or OAuth?

If that question is not confusing to you, just keep on reading.

Whoever asked this question did not understand the idea of OAuth. I wrote a blog post about this topic and explained the difference between LDAP and OAuth. The post[1] still gets new views every day, even after more than two years. It seems to be a hot topic!

If you are new to OAuth or if you have worked with OAuth without needing to understand all the details around it, this section may also help you. To get everyone on the same page I will start with a few terms and how they are used in OAuth!:

- **Resource owner (RO)**: A person, a user, someone who uses an application

- **Client**: An application (app)

- **Access token (AT)**: A short-lived token used by clients to access APIs that require such token as credential. These APIs are referenced as protected resources.

---

[1]"OAuth vs. LDAP," https://communities.ca.com/blogs/oauth/2016/10/18/oauth-vs-ldap

- **Authorization server (AS)**: A server that issues a different OAuth token

- **Resource server (RS)**: A server that provides protected APIs

- **Protected resource (PR)**: An API that serves information about or for the resource owner

- **SCOPE**: Permissions a client is requesting (more details further down)

In general, on a high level, OAuth enables clients to access content on a user's behalf without requiring their credentials. A typical flow in OAuth looks like Figure 5-2. Just follow the flow and pay attention to the question *Who is sharing username, password?*

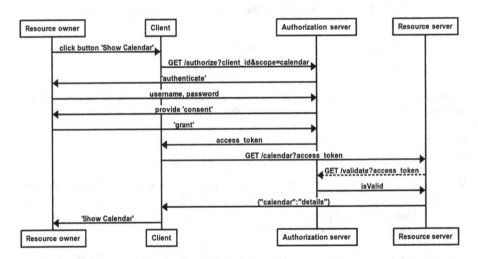

Figure 5-2. *Simple OAuth example*

Figure 5-2 is simplified and introduces a few terms that will be discussed very soon. However, it should provide a glimpse into OAuth flows. Here are the highlights:

- The username and password were only shared between resource owner and authorization server. Neither the client nor the resource server saw those credentials.

- The resource owner was asked to provide his consent! This means that the resource owner was in the position to decide whether the client could access his calendar or not!

- The client received an access_token, which it used with its API request GET /calendar?access_token to the resource server. This was good enough for the resource server to accept the request and return the calendar details {"calendar":"details"}. No user credentials required!

A few years ago, the resource owner would have configured the client with his username and password and the client would have accessed protected resources *impersonating* the resource owner. With OAuth, the client accesses the protected resources *on behalf of* the resource owner!

This was the first flow example, but since OAuth is a framework, it supports other flows too. There are also terms that must be discussed. If you are not interested in knowing the bits and pieces, then at least remember that OAuth is a mechanism for authorizations! If you want to know more, keep on reading.

OAuth, the Details

RFC 6749, OAuth 2.0, is an extensive read and a little confusing. The RFC talks about implicit flows, public clients, refresh_tokens, scope, and a lot of that is not explained in detail. Here are a few fundamental concepts:

- OAuth supports different flows. They are called grant_types.

- A grant_type can be one of the following:

  - authorization_code (CODE)

  - Resource owner password credentials (ROPC)

  - refresh_token (RT)

  - client_credentials (CC)

  - Implicit

- OAuth specifies two types of clients:

  - Public (no, I cannot keep a secret to myself)

  - Confidential (yes, I can keep a secret to myself)

- OAuth specifies two APIs:
  - /authorize (web-based)
  - /token (API-based)
- OAuth matches different flows to different types of clients (applications):
  - JavaScript clients
  - Mobile clients (native implementations)
  - Web applications
- OAuth requires an explicit or implicit consent of resource owners for a client.
- OAuth supports flows that do not involve a resource owner.
  - client_credentials
- OAuth specifies three different types of tokens:
  - access_token
  - refresh_token
  - authorization_code

All of these terms, entities, and descriptions relate to each other. For example, a client that wants to leverage the client_credentials grant_type needs to be of type confidential and will usually be implemented as a web application, or at least on a server and not a mobile device. Figure 5-3 shows the different entities and connects them with each other.

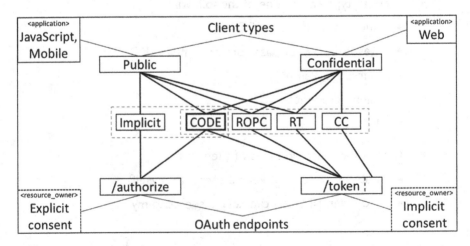

Figure 5-3. *RFC 6749, OAuth 2.0, compact and visualized*

There is a lot going on in Figure 5-3. This is what it says:

- Upper left and right corner:
  - The types of applications relate to client types.
- Lower left and right corner:
  - resource_owners (users) provide an explicit consent, requested during an authorization flow, or implicitly by just using a client.
  - With the client_credentials (cc) flow no user is involved and therefore no consent is required.
- /authorize, /token
  - The two APIs that are specified in OAuth
  - /authorize is used with browser based flows and displays a login and consent screen.
  - /token is used as plain data API; no website is involved.
- Public, Confidential
  - The distinction between clients that are secure and able to keep a secret (confidential) or not (public)
- Implicit
  - A flow that results in a client receiving an access_token
- CODE, ROPC, RT, CC
  - Flows that result in a client receiving an access_token and optionally a refresh_token
- Dotted rectangle surrounding Implicit and CODE
  - Both flows begin with a request to /authorize and involve a browser.
  - Both flows include an initial parameter named response_type (more about that below).
  - In comparison to implicit, CODE receives a temporary token (authorization_code) instead of an access_token. The temporary token has to be exchanged for an access_token in a second step.

- Dotted rectangle surrounding CODE, ROPC, RT, and CC

  - All these flows are API-based with no browser involved.

  - Resource_owners are not required to provide explicit consent. Or they have given it previously.

  - All flows include an initial parameter named grant_ type (more about that below).

Here are a few sample use cases to demonstrate how Figure 5-3 can be used:

1. An application needs to authenticate, but users do not.

2. Users should grant applications explicitly when using the mobile app.

Use the figure this way:

1. **Use case 1**: No user, but the client needs to authenticate ➤ **cc** (client_credentials). From that, you can see that the client type must be **confidential** and should be implemented as **web** application (or at least on a server). The client will use the **/token** endpoint, no consent required.

2. **Use case 2**: Start off in the **explicit consent** corner. Via **/authorize** you get to choose the **implicit** or the **CODE flow. Since the client is mobile, it is also public.**

Now, let's begin discussing flows and all their details! Along the way I will introduce all parameters and hopefully everything that needs to be known about them.

OAuth flows (grant_types)

OAuth supports different flows that clients can choose to obtain authorizations. All flows have a few attributes in common and some specific ones. The common ones are explained in the "General rules" bullet points and specifics are explained within their own section. Whenever anyone starts working with OAuth, they always ask, *Which flow shall I use?* The following sections will explain which one to use and why.

General rules that apply to all flows:

- The /authorize API accepts requests using HTTP GET or POST and always responds with a redirect (HTTP status 302) unless a redirect_uri is not available.

- The /token API only accepts requests using HTTP POST and always responds with content-type **application/json.**

- HTTP POST requests are always used with content-type **application/x-www-form-urlencoded.**

- **HTTPS** is a must!

- For any flow that involves a browser, web-based vulnerabilities have to be addressed.[2]

- Wherever redirect_uris are used, only accept registered ones! Never accept open redirects!

- Submitted parameters must be **URLEncoded**. A typical error is to URLEncode a complete URL instead of just the parameters. It should be done like this:

```
https://example.com/authorize?
```

key1=**urlEncode(value1)**

&key2=**urlEncode(value2)**

instead of

```
https://example.com/authorize?
```

urlEncode(key1=value1&key2=value2)

The examples following here show flows (grant_types) with example configurations. As you get into OAuth, you will discover that any of the following can be used with different parameter values. Nevertheless, to get started, try it as shown for the next five flows, even if the whole section is very technology heavy.

Implicit Grant

Description: A client is requesting an access_token using the response_type *token*. This response_type requires a browser or a web view on a mobile device and prevents the client from accessing the resource owner's credentials. Implicit flows are not secure when it comes to the visibility of issued token. This should only be considered if an exposed access_token is not a risk.

Authorization request:

```
GET /authorize?
client_id={client_id}
&response_type={response_type}
```

---

[2]OAuth related security considerations, https://tools.ietf.org/html/rfc6749#section-10

```
&scope={requested_scope}
&redirect_uri={redirect_uri}
&state={state}
```

Authorization response will be as follows:

```
HTTP status=302
HTTP header 'Location={redirect_uri}
&state={state}
#access_token={access_token}
&expires_in=3600 // lifetime in s, 3600 = default by convention
&token_type=Bearer // other types are optional
&scope={granted_scope}
```

Let's break down the authorization response into its individual components:

- {client_id}: This is a unique identifier that is known at the authorization server and identifies one specific client. It has to be preregistered before it can be used.

- {response_type}: For implicit flows the value is *token* that advises the authorization server to include an access_token in its response.

- {requested_scope}: A client optionally requests scope values. Scope values are specific per environment and are practically permissions. Multiple values may be provided as a space-separated list of values (but URLEncoded!).

- {redirect_uri}: The authorization server will return any error messages or issued token attached to this URL as a URL fragment. The fragment is indicated by the number sign (#). A fragment is only available to the browser! The {redirect_uri} value used in the request must match a pre-registered value. The authorization server will not accept a request if there is a mismatch.

- {state}: An optional state can be included in the request. It is opaque to the authorization server and is meant for the client only. It can be used to prevent CSRF[3] attacks. The authorization server will attach the value as-is to the given redirect_uri in its response.

- {granted_scope}: The authorization server may not grant the requested scope. Therefore, the response includes granted scope.

- {access_token}: The token that can be used by the client to access protected APIs.

---

[3]CSRF in OAuth, https://tools.ietf.org/html/rfc6749#section-10.12

Keep in mind the following danger points:

- Access Token displayed in browser: #access_ token={access_token}

- On mobile devices, a redirect_uri of a third-party-app may be invoked. With that, the token is received by the wrong app!

Authorization_code Grant, Step 1

Description: A client is requesting an access_token using the response_type *code*. This response_type requires a browser or a web view on a mobile device and prevents the client from accessing the resource owner's credentials. This is the most secure response_type when it comes to the visibility of issued tokens. The result is a temporary token, which has to be exchanged for an access_token afterwards (step 2).

Note This is also the flow used for social logins!

Authorization request:

```
GET /authorize?
client_id={client_id}
&response_type={response_type}
&scope={requested_scope}
&redirect_uri={redirect_uri}
&state={state}
```

Authorization response will be as follows. The browser will handle the redirect and forward the URL query parameters to the client:

- HTTP status=302

- HTTP header 'Location={redirect_uri}

  &state={state}

  &code={*authorization_code*} // *difference compared to 'implicit'*

Let's break this down into its components again:

- {response_type}: For the code flow the value is *code*, which advises the authorization server to include an authorization_code in its response.

- {authorization_code}: A temporary token

Keep in mind the following danger points:

- On mobile devices a redirect_uri of a third-party app may be invoked. With that, the authorization_code is received by the wrong app! To mitigate this risk, apply RFC 7636, Proof Key for Code Exchange.[4]

Authorization_code Grant, Step 2

Description: After receiving an authorization_code in Step 1, the client now needs to exchange the code for an access_token.

Authorization request:

```
POST /token
Content-Type: application/x-www-form-urlencoded

client_id={client_id}
&client_secret={client_secret}
&grant_type={grant_type}
&redirect_uri={redirect_uri}
&code={authorization_code}
```

Authorization response includes all issued tokens:

```
HTTP status=200
Content-Type: application/json
{
"access_token":"{access_token}",
  "refresh_token":"{refresh_token}",
  "expires_in": 3600,
  "token_type":"Bearer",
  "scope":"{granted_scope}"
}
```

Here are the components:

- {client_secret}: Just like a password for users, clients have a client_secret.

- {grant_type}: For this flow, the value is *authorization_code*. It advises the authorization server to use the value of code as grant. The authorization server will validate the code and find the associated resource_owner who has granted the client in Step 1.

- {refresh_token}: A second token that can be used by the client to request a new access_token when the first one expires.

---

[4]PKCE explained, https://communities.ca.com/blogs/oauth/2016/11/03/oauth-and-pkce-rfc-7636

- {redirect_uri}: This value has to match the value used in Step 1!

Keep in mind the following danger points:

- One of the few risks is the mix-up problem. This occurs when a client receives an authorization_code from one server but tries to exchange it for an access_token with a fraud server.[5]

Resource Owner Password Credentials (ROPC) Grant

Description: This flow is considered only for trusted clients. The client receives the resource_owner credentials directly. This may be chosen only if the owner of the user credentials (such as an enterprise business) is also the owner of the client (client for employees).

Authorization request:

```
POST /token
Content-Type: application/x-www-form-urlencoded

client_id={client_id}
&client_secret={client_secret}
&grant_type={grant_type}
&username={username}
&password={password}
&scope={requested_scope}
```

Authorization response:

```
HTTP status=200
Content-Type: application/json
{
"access_token":"{access_token}",
  "refresh_token":"{refresh_token}",
  "expires_in": 3600,
  "token_type":"Bearer",
  "scope":"{granted_scope}"
}
```

Let's explain the components again:

- {grant_type}: For this flow the value is *password*. It advises the authorization server to use the provided username and password to authenticate the resource_owner.

---

[5]OAuth Server Metadata, https://tools.ietf.org/html/rfc8414

- {username}: The username of the resource_owner who uses the client
- {password}: The resource_owners password

Keep in mind the following danger points:

- To be used with caution since the client receives the user credentials.

Refresh Token Grant

Description: A client uses a refresh_token to request a new access_ token, optionally a new refresh_token. By design, this token is valid until the resource_owner revokes it. However, many implementations do support an expiration date.

Authorization request:

```
POST /token
Content-Type: application/x-www-form-urlencoded

client_id={client_id}
&client_secret={client_secret}
&grant_type={grant_type}
&refresh_token={refresh_token}
&scope={requested_scope}
```

Authorization response:

```
HTTP status=200
Content-Type: application/json
{
  "access_token":"{access_token}",
  "refresh_token":"{refresh_token}",
  "expires_in": 3600,
  "token_type":"Bearer",
  "scope":"{granted_scope}"
}
```

As usual, the components explained:

- {grant_type}: For this flow the value is *refresh_token*. It advises the authorization server to issue a new token based on the provided refresh_token.
- {refresh_token}: An existing refresh token
- {requested_scope}: The requested scope cannot include any value that has not been requested in the initial authorization request with which the here used refresh_token has been received!

Keep in mind the following danger points:

- Potentially this is a long-lived token. With that, it may be necessary to have resource_owners prove that they are still in possession of the client that received this token from time to time.

Client Credentials Grant

Description: A client requests authorization on its own behalf. No resource_ owner is involved.

Authorization request:

```
POST /token
Content-Type: application/x-www-form-urlencoded

client_id={client_id}
&client_secret={client_secret}
&grant_type={grant_type}
&scope={requested_scope}
```

Authorization response:

```
HTTP status=200
Content-Type: application/json
{
  "access_token":"{access_token}",
  "expires_in": 3600,
  "token_type":"Bearer",
  "scope":"{granted_scope}"
}
```

The grant_type value:

- {grant_type}: For this flow the value is *client_ credentials*. It advises the authorization server to grant authorization on behalf of the client. The client is also the resource_owner.

Keep in mind the following danger points:

- Only confidential clients are supported by this grant type.

These are all flows as specified by RFC 6749. If you are a hardcore OAuth expert, you will notice that I have neglected available options for some flows. For example, alternatively client credentials can be provided as an HTTP header *'Authorization: Basic base64(client_id:client_secret)'* and not as parameters. Nevertheless, I believe the provided descriptions are sufficient in this context.

■ **Tip** You may have observed that these flows often referenced *username, password* as parameters in order to authenticate a resource_owner. Needing to reference username, password is actually only required when the ROPC flow is used! It is not the case for the implicit and CODE flow. Username and password are only used in the RFC and in this chapter because it is the most common way to authenticate users.

I encourage you to choose the best way for your environment to authenticate resource_owners! It may be by cookie, by SAML, by JWT, or a combination of a phone number and an OTP. Whatever it is, do not limit yourself to anything that does not work for your environment. For example, a product I work on issues an authorization_code after resource_owners go through a social login flow with a social platform. No username or password is ever visible in our product, only the code!

OAuth SCOPE

Scope is specified in RFC 6749, but more or less like *scope exists, and it can be used however you want*. The RFC does not specify any values, nor does it provide a good guideline for it. Many questions I get around scope are caused by this openness. But, before you complain and say, *Yes, I have noticed that and it annoys me*, please remember that OAuth is a *framework*! Frameworks usually do not provide details such as specific values. Instead, a framework lets you build whatever you like but within a given and well-known environment. Look at it as a good thing!

In simple words, scope represents permissions. Permissions that enable a client to access protected APIs. And, to be clear, during any OAuth flow, the scope is not directly issued or granted to the client but associated with an issued access_token and refresh_token. A typical example looks like this:

- A client requests authorization, including `scope=read _calendar`.
- An access_token gets issued, associated with `scope=read _calendar`.
- The client uses the access_token at a protected API, which requires the access_token to be associated with that scope.
- The client can read the calendar.

If the same protected API also supports updating a calendar, it may require a second scope for that such as `scope=update_calendar`. The client would have to request that scope additionally, like *scope=read_calendar update_ calendar*. If it tries to update a calendar without having an access_token associated with `scope=update_calendar`, the request will fail!

It is important to remember that scope should be used as permission for clients but not for resource owners! I have often been asked how scope can be issued based on authenticated users that have granted the client. In most cases, the ask is to do it based on certain attributes such as role (i.e. administrator, writer, developer). To be blunt, that is a bad idea!

Let's say an enterprise business has employees and each one has different attributes. OAuth clients are in use and they can access protected APIs. Scope values are specified. To manage all of these entities, a few components are required:

- *Employees*: Employees are managed in an LDAP server.

- *Employee attributes*: Attributes are managed in an LDAP server.

- *OAuth clients*: Clients are managed in a database or and LDAP server.

- *SCOPE*: Scope values are managed in a database or an LDAP server.

- *APIs*: APIs are managed in an API Portal system.

These entities need to be put into a relation with each other. This is how it should be:

- API requires scope; scope is granted to clients.

- API requires attributes; attributes are assigned to resource owners.

Timewise it should like this:

- During the authorization request:

  - Grant scope based on client.

- When a protected API is accessed:

  - API checks for scope.

  - API checks for attributes of resource_owner.

Using this approach does not tie together scope and resource_owner attributes.

If the other approach is taken, issuing scope based on clients and resource_ owner attributes, they are suddenly tied together. Doing that creates a system where scope is practically an additional attribute for resource_ owners rather than a permission for clients! The same flow as before would now look like this:

- During the authorization request:
  - Grant scope based on client.
  - Grant scope based on resource_owner.
- When a protected API is accessed:
  - API checks for scope.

Enabling this does not only imply that all scopes are assigned to clients and resource owners. It also implies that the authorization server is able to know which APIs will be accessed by the client. That is often not the case! A client may be able to access the API /calendar but also /email. Both APIs may use the same scope's *read write update*.

Unfortunately, a typical authorization request does not include the information of which API will be accessed. The only parameter that could be used is scope. But now scope values cannot be reused for different APIs! It will cause a huge maintenance challenge! The two APIs would now need their own scopes such as read_email write_email update_email. And if you assume that those APIs have multiple versions it introduces another level of scope complexity.

With that in mind, do not try to use scope for anything else than client permissions. An API should always know which scopes it requires and, in addition, and only if needed, which resource_owner attributes need to be available. Here is an example:

- The application CalendarClient is used by owners of a calendar but also by administrators.
- The protected API to access a calendar supports these features:
  - Read a calendar: scope=read
  - Update a calendar: scope=update
  - Delete a calendar: scope=delete
  - Update other calendar: scope=write_other
    - This scope enables a client to update a calendar of other resource_owners.

- The client CalendarClient is used by any employee and always requests the same scope: scope=read update delete write_other.

- The authorization server authenticates the client and the resource_owner, and issues those scopes. This means the authorization only checks these conditions:

  - Valid client requesting valid scope?

  - Valid user?

  - Both validations successful? → issue access_token

    The authorization server does not know (and does not care) which protected APIs will be accessed later!

- The calendar API, however, implements this logic:

  - For all operations, it will check if the required scope is associated with the given access_token.

  - For any non-read operation, it will also check if the associated resource_owner is also the owner of the accessed calendar! This is not based on scope but is based on attributes. No other user than the owner should be able to modify the calendar.

  - In addition, the API has implemented support for writing onto other calendars if the associated resource_owner is an administrator. This is also based on attributes.

To decide how OAuth clients, scopes, resource_owners, and APIs are related to each other, do not hesitate to take the team and simulate different approaches. Make sure team members of different groups within the organization are involved!

On a big side note, be conscious about naming conventions and remember that most resource_owners do not know what scope is. And they should not have to know. If your team implements a Consent page that displays requested scope values (permissions), make sure to not display the scope value by itself! In most cases, that will be perceived as completely useless and confusing.

For example, your Consent page should not display this:

- Client xyz requests SCOPE: *read update delete* to manage your calendar.

Instead it should display this:

- Client xyz would like to manage your calendar.

Scope should always be represented as a human-readable message!

OAuth Consent

One reason why OAuth became popular is the fact that resource_owners are put in control of who can access their data. Most likely anybody reading this book has been in front of a screen that displayed something like this: "Application xyz would like to access your email address. Do you grant this request?" This is the point in time where a click on Grant or Deny shows the power any user has. Clicking Deny simply rejects the wish of an application. No administrator or any other entity can overrule the decision.

Although this is very good, there is something that has not been supported so far, at least not in a larger scale. Whenever a user clicks Grant, there has been no specified location where this decision could have been viewed. Sure, some applications have a section within a user profile saying "Associated applications" or similar. But there is no standardized way of supporting this kind of feature.

In recent months the term "consent receipt" has been brought up often, especially during the introduction of GDPR[6] in Europe. It's exactly what it is called: a receipt for any given consent. This came up first (as far as I know) at the workshop "Internet Identity Workshop (IIW)" in Mountain View, California in October, 2015[7]. The concept is similar to a receipt you get after purchasing an item in a store. It states clearly what has been purchased when and where. It can be used to prove that this event happened.

In the world of OAuth, the receipt could look like this:

Consent receipt	
Application:	API Book Consent Receipt App
Date:	10. June 2018, 13:10:00 PST
Permissions:	read write update
Domain:	example.com
Expiration:	unlimited, revocation required
URL:	https://example.com/consent
Reason:	Required as an example
Status:	Active

---

[6]GDPR, www.eugdpr.org
[7]Consent receipt at IIW, http://iiw.idcommons.net/Consent_Receipts_in_UMA

It is more important than ever to enable any resource_owner to find an overview of receipts. And, as a vital feature, let resource_owner revoke a consent but without removing the history of such events!

The receipt above could change its state from Active to Revoked when resource_owner decided to revoke access for the associated client.

OAuth and Step-Up Authentication

Let me answer this question first:

What is step-up authentication?

In general, it means requiring a stronger credential than have been provided in the past. If a user has been authenticated by username and password, step-up may mean providing a one-time-password or answering questions x, y, and z. Step-up is usually defined within a specific domain.

Despite that fact that OAuth by itself has no such concept as step-up authentication, I have been in many meetings about this topic. Most meetings asked the question *when* to require step-up authentication: during the initial authentication (when granting a client) or at the point in time when a specific API gets accessed?

I always look at it this way: If you want to know if a resource_owner is the one who pretends who he is when it comes to transferring one million dollar, you want the step-up authentication to happen the moment where the money is transferred!

Here is an example.

A system provides two APIs:

- API: /transfer
    - Moves funds from one account to another
- API: /stepup
    - Authenticates resource_owners

A resource_owner has been authenticated during an authorization request using username and password. Now, the same resource_owner clicks a button in his client named Transfer and the amount is $1,000,000. This is what happens:

1. Client request:

    POST /transfer

    Authorization: Bearer {access_token}

    Content-Type: application/x-www-form-urlencoded

    `amount=1000000&from_account=111&to_account=222`

2. API:

    /transfer: the API validates the incoming request. It realizes that the original authentication statement of the resource_owner, who is associated with the given access_token, is more than 15 minutes old and has an authentication class reference (acr)[8] value of 1 but it requires 3! It returns this response, requiring a new, stronger authentication:

    HTTP status: 401 (authentication required)

3. The client receives the response and redirects the resource_owner to /stepup.

4. API:

    /stepup: It requests a resource_owner to provide a username, password, and an OTP (one-time password), which has been send to his mobile device. Once the resource_owner confirms the OTP, the client redirects him back to /transfer, using the same values as before.

5. API:

    /transfer: The validation of the incoming request now succeeds, and the amount can be transferred from one account to another.

If the same step-up authentication had been required during the initial authorization flow, there would be no guarantee that the authenticated user is still the same when the amount of $1,000,000 got transferred.

As a hint, keep this in mind:

Require step-up authentication as close to the requiring event as possible!

Although OAuth by itself has nothing to do with step-up authentication, it may still be related to it!

---

[8]ACR in ISO, www.iso.org/standard/45138.html

JWT (JSON Web Token)

The book early on referenced JWT but did not explain what it is. The next section introduces id_token. Before I continue, I would like to explain how JWT and id_token look and how they relate to each other. That should make it easier to follow the next few pages.

A JWT is a set of claims represented as a JSON message and encoded in a JSON Web Signature (JWS[9]) and/or JSON Web Encryption (JWE[10]). This representation enables digital signatures and encryption. Once serialized to a string, it consists of three base64url encoded sections, separated by a dot (.). See the following example:

eyJhbGciOiJIUzI1NiIsInR5cCI6IkpXVCJ9.eyJzdWIiOiIxMjM0NTY3ODkwIiwibm
FtZSI6IkpvaG4gRG9lIiwiaWF0IjoxNTE2MjM5MDIyfQ.SflKxwRJSMeKKF2QT4fwp
MeJf36POk6yJV_adQssw5

The sections of the string are as follows:

- JWT header ({from zero to first dot}.)

  - eyJhbGciOiJIUzI1NiIsInR5cCI6IkpXVCJ9

  - base64 decoded: `{"alg":"HS256","typ":"JWT"}`

- JWT payload (.{between the two dots}.)

  - eyJzdWIiOiIxMjM0NTY3ODkwIiwibmFtZSI
    6IkpvaG4gRG9lIiwiaWF0IjoxNTE2MjM5MDIyfQ

  - base64 decoded: `{"sub":"1234567890","name":
    "John Doe","iat":1516239022}`

- JWT signature (.{after the last dot to the end of the string})

  - SflKxwRJSMeKKF2QT4fwpMeJf36POk6yJV_adQssw5

This simple format enables JWT to be exchanged as an HTTP parameter or header, although they are not bound to HTTP! Generally, JWT may be used in any context. JWTs are also not bound to protocols or frameworks such as OpenID Connect or OAuth. On the other hand, the usage of JWT in OAuth and OpenID Connect are reasons for their wide adoption.

---

[9]JWS, JSON Web Signature, https://tools.ietf.org/html/rfc7515
[10]JWE, JSON Web Encryption, https://tools.ietf.org/html/rfc7516

If you are now wondering *When and where shall I use a JWT?*, here are a few use cases:

- Message integrity:
    - A message is communicated between party A and C via B. Party B should not be able to manipulate the message. Therefore, party A creates a JWS using a shared secret. Party C can validate the integrity.
    - Example: An application supports financial transactions that include a currency, an amount, and a recipient. It is important that none of those values can be manipulated.
- Message confidentiality:
    - A message is communicated between party A and C via B, Party B should not be able to read the message. Therefore, party A creates a JWE using party C's public key. Party C can decrypt and read the message, but party B cannot.
    - Example: An application communicates health data between different parties. Only authorized ones should be able to read the messages.

JWS and JWE both support shared secrets and public/private keys. Shared secrets have to be exchanged via a secure method which, unfortunately, is not specified in the RFCs. Nevertheless, in OAuth and OpenID Connect the *OAuth client_secret* is usually used for this purpose. For public/private keys, the JWT header may contain complete certificate chains or references to used keys. This information can be used by recipients to determine which key to use for validation purposes. For a list of all header values, refer to RFC 7515, section 4[11].

Next, I will explain what id_token is and after that how JWT, JWS, and id_token work together.

id_token

id_tokens are JSON messages with a well-defined list of keys (set of claims). Each key within the id_token is defined in the OpenID Connect Core specification[12]. Some keys are mandatory, and others are optional. Table 5-1 gives an overview with a short explanation. Full details can be viewed directly in the referenced specification.

---

[11]JOSE headers, https://tools.ietf.org/html/rfc7515#section-4
[12]id_token, http://openid.net/specs/openid-connect-core-1_0.html#IDToken

Table 5-1. Overview of id_token keys

Key	Example	Required	Short description
iss	https://server.example.com	true	**Issuer:** The issuing entity. Usually a valid URL.
sub	24400320	true	Subject: Either a username or a ppid (pairwise pseudonymous identifier)
aud	s6BhdRkqt3	true	**Audience:** The audience for whom this id_token is intended for. A client_id of the requesting client. Optionally other audiences.
exp	1530774920	true	**Expiration:** The 10-digit Unix timestamp (seconds since 01-01-1970) when this token expires
iat	1530772920	true	Issued at: The 10-digit Unix timestamp when this token was issued
auth_time	1530772120	false	Authentication time: The 10-digit Unix timestamp when the resource_owner was authenticated
nonce	a-ranD8m-4alue	false	A client-side value, opaque to the server. It is available only if the client included it in its authorization request.
acr	http://fo.example.com/loa-1	false	Authentication Context Class Reference, specifying the LoA (Level of Assurance) of the authentication
amr	otp pwd	false	Authentication Methods Reference: A reference to the method of authentication
azp	s6BhdRkqt3	false	Authorized Party: The client_id of the requesting client

The highlighted keys (Issuer, Audience, Expiration) are the ones that are always relevant when validating id_token. Others may be neglected in simple use cases.

Since id_tokens are also JWT, they are expressed as JWS. With that, they are URL friendly and integrity protected! Because of that, id_token and JWT often refer to each other. But keep this in mind:

id_tokens are just one type of JWT!

Creating an id_token (JWT)

id_token includes the keys (or claims) shown above. Optionally, details of resource_owners, such as preferred_username or email, are also included. The OP will do the following:

- Create the JWT header:
  - {"typ":"jwt", "alg":"HS256"}: Indicates the usage of a shared secret using the algorithm HMAC-SHA256. The receiving party has to be informed which shared secret to use for the signature validation.
  - {"typ":"jwt", "alg":"RS256", "kid":"d273113ad205"}: Indicates the usage of a private key using the algorithm RSASSA-PKCS1-v1_5 SHA-256. For validations the receiving party has to use the public key referenced as d273113ad205.
- Create the payload:
  - This is the id_token
- Create the signature:
  - Create the input:
    - Input = base64urlEncode(jwt-header). base64urlEncode(jwt-payload)
  - Sign the input:
    - JWT-signature = base64urlEncode(sign (alg, input))
- Serialize the output (referred to as JWS Compact Serialization):
  - jwt.compact = input. signature

The string jwt.compact can now be returned to a requesting client. The process of validating the JWT will be discussed later.

OpenID Connect

OpenID Connect is referenced as *identity layer on top of OAuth 2.0*. It adds the missing link between an OAuth application and resource_owners. In particular, it enables developers to implement applications that are aware of the current resource_owner. It also supports identity federation between different parties.

Why OpenID Connect?

In cases where OAuth is used with a response_type (requests send to the OAuth /authorize API), clients are generally not able to retrieve details of the resource_owner. Clients are not able to display a message such as *Hello Sascha!* Regardless of that, it is often desired. To bypass this limitation (or better, *that part of OAuth's privacy model*) applications have implemented proprietary OAuth-protected APIs that simply return those details. In order to access those details, resource_owners must grant permissions (scope) that are also proprietary.

This situation did not make developers lives easier! For example, if a developer wanted to build an application that retrieved user details at two different platforms, he had to use different SCOPE values and different APIs that produced different responses. In one case, it could have been SCOPEs such as wl.basic, wl.emails; in the other case, user_about_me, email. In one case, the API would have been /user; in the other case /me. And with that, responses were different, too.

After some time, the OpenID Foundation[13] took on the task of creating a specification to align all those different efforts that were around. OpenID Connect, as an *identity layer on top of OAuth*, was born!

How Does It Work?

Simply said, OpenID Connect uses OAuth, just like other applications. Before I discuss the details, here is the high-level flow:

1. Request an access_token granted for specific SCOPEs.

2. Send an OAuth request to the resource_server and receive the resource_owner's details.

That's it, on a high level! On a lower level, there are many details around it. But first things first.

OpenID Connect started off with a few main features in the Core[14] specification (also referred to as the Basic profile[15]):

- Formalized OAuth SCOPE

  - openid, email, profile, address, phone,

---

[13]OpenID Foundation, http://openid.net
[14]OpenID Connect, Core, http://openid.net/specs/openid-connect-core-1_0.html
[15]OpenID Connect, Basic profile, http://openid.net/wordpress-content/uploads/2018/06/OpenID-Connect-Conformance-Profiles.pdf

- Formalized userinfo API that returns details about the resource_owner

  - /userinfo, request, and response

- Introduced a token, identifying an authenticated resource_owner

  - id_token (JSON message with well-defined structure)

- Introduced and extended OAuth response_types

  - response_type=token id_token

  - response_type=code // this exists in OAuth, but in combination with SCOPE=openid the token response includes an id_token

  - Additional response_types were added too, but not right from the beginning

This list may look short, but it simplified the development of applications! Here are the reasons:

- For each SCOPE, OpenID Connect has specified a list of claims[16] that may be returned. This enables a developer to implement an application that can handle responses of different platforms with one code base.

- The way to invoke the /userinfo API is always the same. The response is always the same: a JSON message with a well-defined structure.

- The id_token is a JWT and is expressed as a JWS and can be validated by the client without having to send a validation request to the issuing server.

- The different response_types allow clients to choose the desired flow, depending on their use case.

An authorization request always starts off at the OAuth /authorize API. Here is a simple example:

GET/authorize?client_id=...&redirect_uri=...&state=astatevalue&...

...scope=openid+email+profile&response_type=token+id_token

---

[16]OpenID Connect, Claims, http://openid.net/specs/openid-connect-core-1_0. html#StandardClaims

The SCOPE and response_type values influence the response as follows:

- **SCOPE openid:** The client indicates to the server that it is requesting an OpenID Connect flow. Look at this value as kind of a switch, as in *OpenID Connect on/ off.* If it is not included, any of the other SCOPE values will be treated as non-OpenID Connect values. Some server implementations may even fail the request. The response will include the claim *sub*, which contains the username as plain text or a ppid, which is expressed as opaque string

- **SCOPE profile:** The client is requesting general information about the resource_owner such as *name, family_name, given_name, preferred_username.*

- **SCOPE email:** The client is requesting the email address of the resource_owner. The response will also include the claim *email_verified.* This indicates that the responding platform can confirm that this email address is a valid one.

- **Response_type token id_token:** token is known from OAuth that indicates an *implicit* flow. The server will respond with an OAuth access_token. In addition, an id_token will be issued. This token cannot be used at any protected API. Instead, it represents an authenticated user.

Based on the example request above, the following responses will be received:

- Response from /authorize would include this in the redirect_uri:

  - **...#access_token=...&id_token=eyJh... ssw5c&...**

- Response from the /userinfo API could look like this:

  - {"sub": "12ab34cd56ef","preferred_ username": "saspr","name": "Sascha Preibisch","email": "sascha@example. com","email_verified": true}

Although the early version of the Core specification already simplified the life for application developers, many more features were added over time. Nowadays the OpenID Connect ecosystem is a very comprehensive list of specifications including a self-service testing system. The next section explains how to find the way through the specifications, with a focus on authentication and authorization.

How to Leverage OpenID Connect

Within API ecosystems OAuth is a common participant of authorization flows. In addition, OpenID Connect is the de facto standard for the authentication part. For example, wherever a web site provides a button like "Log in with Google" or "Log in with Facebook", an OpenID Connect flow gets initiated[17]. Not only can applications design the onboarding process for new users easier this way, they can also reduce the number of times a login and consent screen are displayed.

Before supporting or leveraging OpenID Connect, it has to be decided which role the system is taking on:

- OP: OpenID Provider (server)
- RP: Relying Party (client)

An OP is an OAuth server that also supports OpenID Connect features. Clients may connect to the server and use extended OAuth responses_types such as token id_token. RP registers itself as an OAuth client at the OP and uses an OpenID Connect-enabled OAuth flow to authenticate resource_owners. Any system may take on both roles, too.

As an OP, a few use cases are more dominant than others. Here are the ones I get asked about most:

1. Take resource_owners through an initial login and consent flow.

2. During consecutive authorization flows, display the login screen only if the resource_owner has no session and do not display the consent screen again.

3. Accept an id_token issued by a third party as resource_owner credentials.

OpenID Connect has many more features, but these three seem to be of the biggest interest. Therefore, I will explain how they are used.

Use Case 1: Take resource_owners Through an Initial Login and Consent Flow

This is straightforward. A resource_owner uses a client to access a protected resource. The client's implementation requires the resource_owner to be logged in. The client initiates an authorization flow using response_type=code.

---

[17]Example, social login flow, https://youtu.be/0b0D5ZCFKnc

The flow redirects the resource_owner to the OP, which provides a login and consent screen. Once the resource_owner got authenticated and has authorized the client, an authorization_code gets issued. All of this is standard OAuth.

There is just one value that makes the difference compared to a default authorization request: SCOPE:

- ...&scope=openid+email+profile&...

The difference is not the parameter itself, but the content. If you read the previous section around OAuth, you will note that otherwise nothing special can be seen here. Nevertheless, the OP has to take care of this task:

- **IF** SCOPE contains (*openid*) **THEN** persist the consent decision and issue an *id_token* in addition to other token such as access_token and refresh_token.

This task is emphasized because it is important for the three listed use cases above. The OP may receive other parameters, but they are not relevant for this discussion. As a final outcome, the client will not only receive the default token response but also the issued id_token. With that, the resource_owner is *logged in*. The client now may send a request to the OP's /userinfo API to receive resource_owner details.

Use Case 2: During Consecutive Authorization Flows Display the Login Screen Only If the resource_owner Has No Session and Do Not Display the Consent Screen Again

This use case has several aspects to it. For one, the login screen should be displayed only if no session exists. A session is identified by an active id_token. Furthermore, the consent screen should not be displayed again! Not again means it is independent of an existing session and has to be managed as its own entity!

So, how do these requirements work together?

OpenID Connect has introduced a few more parameters[18] compared to default OAuth. For this example, we are looking at a few of them:

- prompt: This may contain one or multiple values.
  - none: Do not display a login and consent screen.
  - login: Prompt for login.

---

[18]OpenID Connect parameters, http://openid.net/specs/openid-connect-core-1_0.html#AuthRequest

- *consent*: Prompt for consent.

- *select_account*: Enable the resource_owner to select an account. This is useful for users with multiple accounts.

- *id_token_hint*: This contains a single value.

  - *id_token*: The id_token that was issued earlier.

These parameters can be used by the client whenever it requires a new access_token. This would be the case where its access_token and refresh_token have expired. A typical client implementation would look as shown in Figure 5-4, simplified.

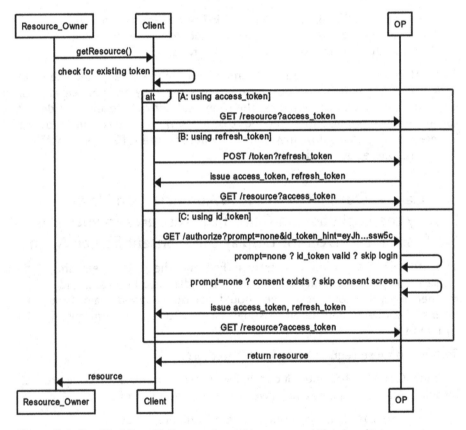

Figure 5-4. Simplified OpenID Connect flow with prompt and id_token_hint parameters

The diagram has three alternatives:

1. The client uses an existing access_token to access a protected resource. The OP validates the token and returns the requested resource.

2. The client's access_token has expired and therefore it uses its refresh_token to request new token. The OP validates the refresh_token and issues a new access_token and refresh_token. The client uses the new access_token and retrieves the resource.

3. Both tokens have expired, access_token and refresh_token. This is the case that is different from default OAuth. Without OpenID Connect, the client would now need to request new tokens by taking the resource_owner through a new authorization flow, which would prompt for login and consent. But, instead the client leverages the additional parameters prompt and id_token_hint. By setting prompt=none the client indicates to the OP *do not display any screens to my user!* Needless to say, OP still has to validate the request:

    a. To skip the login screen:

        i. Is the id_token still valid?

        ii. Fail otherwise

    b. To skip the consent screen:

        i. Does the requested SCOPE match the previously issued SCOPE, or a subset?

        ii. Did the resource_owner provide consent previously for this client?

        iii. Fail otherwise

Using this feature reduces the times a user gets confronted with login and/or consent screens. This not only improves the user experience but also reduces the number of times a resource_owner has to use his password! Each time the password does not need to be used is a step towards password-less systems.

Use Case 3: Accept a id_token Issued by a Third Party as resource_owner Credentials

Federation is one of the biggest features in OpenID Connect! There even is a new, dedicated specification for it: *OpenID Connect Federation 1.0 – draft 05*[19], currently in a draft status (October 2018). The specification will evolve over the next few months. But even without that specification, federation can be supported.

Federation in OpenID Connect is based on id_token. Since id_tokens are JWT, any recipient can validate them by verifying the signature. A typical validation process includes these steps:

1. Verify the issuer as an accepted third party.
2. Verify the expiration date.
3. Verify the signature algorithm.
4. Verify the signature.

■ **Important** Bullet point 3 is extremely important! Never validate a JWT by using the *alg* value of the JWT header. It could have been replaced with any other algorithm by a third party and therefore the message integrity cannot be assumed!

Validating id_token in Detail

As mentioned, there are several signature algorithms available. In the case of HS256, the OP and RP usually agree on using the client_secret for creating and validating the signature. There is hardly a question on how to distribute that value.

Nevertheless, in a system that leverages RS256 or ES256 it becomes more complicated. OpenID Connect has invested quite some effort into the process of simplifying and normalizing the validation. The effort resulted in additional specifications and APIs:

- OpenID Connect Discovery[20]
  - A specification describing a discovery document (JSON) that lists features that are supported.
  - It's list of APIs, supported response_types, SCOPEs, and other details.

---

[19]OpenID Connect Federation, https://openid.net/specs/openid-connect-federation-1_0.html
[20]OpenID Connect Discovery, http://openid.net/specs/openid-connect-discovery-1_0.html

- /.well-known/openid-configuration

  - The API returning the discovery document

- /jwks.json

  - The API containing a list of JSON Web Keys (more or less the public certificates required for RS and ES-based signature algorithms)

OpenID Provider

The validation process starts at the OP. The OP prepares his system in such a way that any RP can validate JWT issued by the OP. These are the steps required by an OP:

1. iss (issuer)

   a. The OP publishes its iss value. This can be a URL.

   b. By specification, this URL does not need to be resolvable, but in my experience, this is usually the case.

   c. iss itself has to appear in the OpenID Connect Discovery document (issuer).

   d. Ideally this value is the only one a RP needs to configure!

2. /.well-known/openid-configuration

   a. The OP configures all details of its system that should be publicly available.

   b. This URL is standardized. RP should be able to use it like this:

      i. {iss}/.well-known/openid-configuration

3. /jwks.json

   a. The OP configures this API to return a list of public keys that are used for JWT signatures.

   b. The keys are expressed as JSON Web Key Set (JWK/JWKS[21]).

   c. Each key is identified by a key ID (kid).

   d. When the OP issues an id_token (JWT) the JWT header needs to include the matching kid!

---

[21] JSON Web Key, https://tools.ietf.org/html/rfc7517

Here are example documents.

The response of /.well-known/openid-connect:

```
{ "authorization_endpoint": "https://example.com/op/server/auth/oauth/v2/
authorize", "token_endpoint": "https://example.com/op/server/auth/oauth/v2/
token", "jwks_uri": "https://example.com/op/server/jwks.json",
"response_types_supported": ["code", "id_token", "code id_token", "id_token
token"], "scopes_supported": ["openid", "profile", "email"],
"issuer": "https://example.com/op/server",
...}
```

The response of /jwks.json:

```
{ "keys": [{
"kty": "RSA",
"use": "sig",
"kid": "d273113ad205",
"x5c": ["MIIDBTCCA...c5194bcc59"]}]
}
```

After the OP has prepared its environment, it can start issuing id_token (JWT).

Relying Party

Interested RPs will now prepare their own environments:

1. Configure accepted *iss.*

    a. The RP configures its application to accept only JWT
        issued by one or multiple configured parties, such as
        `https://example.com/op/server` or `https://
        anotherone.com/op/server`.

    b. Only accept the HTTPS scheme. Fail otherwise!

2. Configure expected `alg`.

    a. As mentioned before, **NEVER** trust the `alg` found in
        the JWT header!

That's it!

The next step is to implement the validation flow that starts after receiving
the id_token (JWT). There are many steps required but once implemented it
is actually straightforward. The flow should execute CPU (calculate signature)
and latency (network calls) heavy operations late in the process:

1. Base64 decode the JWT-payload (the part between the two dots).

2. Extract `iss` and compare the value against a configured, acceptable one.

3. Extract `exp` and check that it has not expired.

4. Extract `aud` and check if the client_id is included.

   a. This may be skipped for federation cases.

5. Base64 decode the JWT-header and check if at least `kid`, `alg`, and `typ` are included.

   a. `alg` has to match the expected value.

   b. Fail otherwise!

6. Retrieve the discovery document:

   a. GET {iss}/.well-known/openid-configuration

7. Extract the jwks URL (`jwks_url`) as found in the discovery document.

8. Retrieve the JWKS.

   a. GET {`jwks_url`}

   b. Only accept the HTTPS scheme. Fail otherwise!

9. Find a `kid` that matches the one found in the JWT-header.

   a. Fail if there is none!

10. Extract the associated JWK and use it to validate the JWT signature.

    a. Recreate the signature and compare it to the given one.

    b. Fail if it does not match!

These ten steps are required for the validation process. Figure 5-5 displays the steps on a high level.

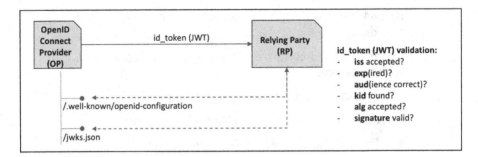

Figure 5-5. High-level id_token (JWT) validation process

Any other validation is most likely application specific.

OAuth vs. OpenID Connect vs. LDAP

This content is based on one of my blog posts. I decided to include it in this book and within this chapter because this topic causes a lot of confusion according to questions I have received in the past. It relates to API design and can be seen as an add-on to the last section.

To set the stage, here are a few short descriptions to remember:

- If OAuth is a set of characters, OpenID Connect creates words and a language using them.

- OpenID Connect is a profile on top of OAuth just like HTTP is on top of TCP.

- OAuth knows about apps; OpenID Connect knows about users.

Let's get started!

LDAP (Lightweight Directory Access Protocol)

A LDAP server (full disclosure: I am not an expert on LDAP) is a directory structure that contains details and attributes about users. It may contain a username, firstname, lastname, password (or the hash of a password), addresses, certificates, date of birth, roles—all kinds of stuff. The data of an LDAP gets accessed for different purposes:

- To authenticate a user: Compare the given username and password against values found in the LDAP.

- To retrieve attributes: Retrieve firstname, lastname, role for a given username.

- To authorize users: Retrieve access rights for directories for a given username.

I believe that most developers at some point in time have to deal with an LDAP server. I also believe that most developers will agree with what I just described.

OAuth

OAuth is a framework that enables applications (clients) to gain access to resources without receiving any details of the users they are being used by. To make it a little more visual I will introduce an example.

The very cool app named FancyEMailClient

In the old days,

- For each email provider, the user provides details such as smtp server, pop3 server, username, password on a configuration page within *FancyEMailClient.*

- *FancyEMailClient* now accesses all configured email accounts on behalf of the user. More precise, *FancyEMailClient* is acting **AS** the user!

- The user has shared all details with *FancyEMailClient.* I must say, it feels a little fishy; don't you agree?

In the days of OAuth:

- *FancyEMailClient* is an OAuth client and gets registered at each email provider that should be supported.

- *FancyEMailClient* does not ask users for any email provider details whatsoever.

- *FancyEMailClient* delegates authentication and authorization to the selected email provider via a redirect_uri.

- *FancyEMailClient* retrieves an access_token and uses this token at an API such as /provider/email to retrieve the user's emails. The access_token may be granted for scope=email_api.

- *FancyEMailClient* has no clue who the user is and has not seen any details such as username or password.

- This is perfect in regard to the user's privacy needs. However, *FancyEMailClient* would like to display a message such as "Hello Sascha" if Sascha is the user, but it can't.

OpenID Connect

As I explained above, a client does not get any details about the resource_ owner. But, since most applications would at least like to display a friendly message such as "Hello Sascha" there needs to be something to help them.

To stick to the email provider example, before OpenID Connect (OIDC) was born, these providers simply created OAuth-protected APIs (resources) that would return details about the resource_owner. Users would first give their consent and afterwards the client would get the username or firstname and would display "Hello Sascha."

Since this became a requirement for almost any OAuth client, we now have a common way of doing that, specified in OpenID Connect. OIDC has specified SCOPE values, a /userinfo API, and an id_token that represents an authenticated user.

In order to enhance the OAuth version of *FancyEMailClient*, the developer of it would only have to do a few little tweaks:

1. When requesting access to emails, also request access to user details. The request would now have to include something like ...&scope=openid+profile+email+em ail_api&... (scope == permissions like access control).

2. During the authentication and authorization flow, the user would not only grant access to his emails but also to his personal details.

3. *FancyEMailClient* would now receive an access_token that could not only be used at /provider/email but also at /provider/userinfo.

4. *FancyEMailClient* can now display "Hello Sascha!"

Now the big question: How does it all come together?

LDAP servers are the only component that exists without OAuth and OpenID Connect. LDAP servers are always the source of users (and maybe also clients and other entities). LDAP servers have always been used to authenticate users and have been leveraged to authorize them for accessing resources. OAuth and OpenID Connect can't be supported if no LDAP server is available. OAuth and OpenID Connect are protocols only, not systems to manage users.

Figure 5-6 shows an example system.

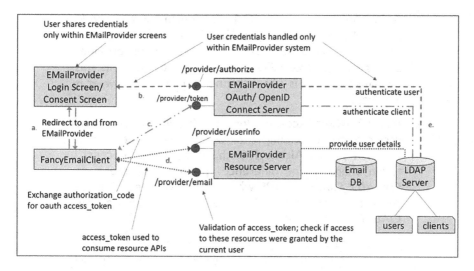

Figure 5-6. OAuth and OpenID Connect-based authentication/authorization

Here is how *FancyEMailClient* works using the different technologies.

Case: OAuth

Here is how *FancyEMailClient* works using OAuth.

a. When a user selects an email provider within *FancyEMailClient*, his browser gets redirected to that provider. It is an **OAuth authorization request** and includes OAuth SCOPE values. To access the API / provider/email, a SCOPE value such as email_api may be included. I say "may" because there is no standard SCOPE for that. To also gain access to the user details, other SCOPE values need to be included. This is more straightforward since they have been specified within **OpenID Connect**. An openid profile email would be sufficient and is supported by practically all OIDC providers. In the end of the flow, *FancyEMailClient* gets back an **OAuth authorization_code**.

b. The user only shares his credentials with EMailProvider. He types them into the EMailProvider's login page and EMailProvider will validate them against his **LDAP server**. (The LDAP server may be a database or any other system that maintains user details.)

c. After receiving the **OAuth authorization_code** *FancyEMailClient* exchanges this short-lived token for an **OAuth access_token**. That access_token provides access to resource APIs. I hope it is obvious that this exchange request is a backchannel request; no browser is involved!

d. *FancyEMailClient* accesses /provider/email and /provider/ userinfo by providing the **OAuth access_token** it received earlier. Although both APIs require an access_ token, there is one difference. /provider/userinfo is an **OpenID Connect API** whereas /provider/email is an API proprietary to the EMailProvider. Let's call it a plain OAuth-protected API.

e. In this area I want to emphasize the role of the **LDAP server**. As you can see, it is involved during almost all requests.

Case: The Old Days

The same app without using OAuth would probably look something like shown in Figure 5-7.

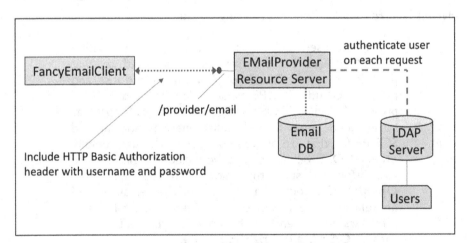

Figure 5-7. Good old authentication

A user would share his credentials with *FancyEMailClient*. And he would do this for each single provider he had an account with. *FancyEMailClient* would probably also ask for other details so that an API such as /provider/userinfo would not even be necessary. *FancyEMailClient* would now collect all this sensitive data and could do whatever it wants with it. That is a big disadvantage!

Another disadvantage is the fact that the user's credentials are now used for each single request. This increases the chances for them being exposed.

OAuth, OpenID Connect, and LDAP are connected with each other. But I hope it becomes obvious which component plays which role and that one cannot replace the other. You may say that my explanation is very black and white, but I hope that it clarifies the overall situation.

Summary

This chapter discussed questions that come up in the context of API-based authentication and authorization and gave an introduction to patterns that should be avoided or explicitly addressed.

Authentication and authorization were discussed and distinguished from each other. You should now be able to decide at which point in message flows authentication and authorization should be handled.

API Implementation Details

After discussing some important points about APIs in general, this chapter will walk through different aspects of API implementations. Everything discussed here is based around typical, real-world requirements that I have observed over the last few years. Even if you are not a developer, this information will help you. All team members should have the same understanding of what should be found within an API.

Before we get into the subject, here are a few terms with an explanation of how they are used. This is to get all audiences onto the same page.

- **Client**: Application or app
- **User**: Resource owner or person
- **Device**: A phone or tablet or computer in general
- **Entity**: All of those above

It is necessary to understand and distinguish these terms. It happens too often that, for example, within a telephone conference someone talks about what *the client is doing* and one group assumes it is a user, but others have an application on their mind!

© CA 2018
S. Preibisch, *API Development*, https://doi.org/10.1007/978-1-4842-4140-0_6

In general, any meeting should introduce the terminology as used in its context!

API Protection: Controlling Access

Every API needs some kind of protection. Even if an API is made to only return the current time, it could still be overloaded and bring down a server. And, if bringing down a server is not a concern, protection could also refer to logging the usage of it. However, in the context of this chapter, *protection* describes how valid entities can be identified and how to prevent APIs from being overloaded.

Have a look at Figure 6-1. It displays relevant attributes that can be extracted from the network- or message-level space of any request. At this moment, do not worry about terms you don't know, This is meant to give you an overview of information that is available and can be used to implement different means of protection.

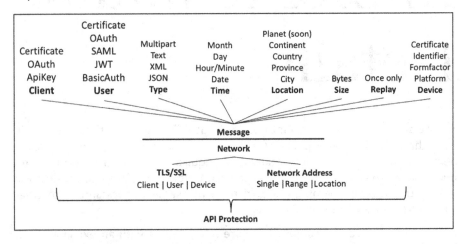

Figure 6-1. Overview of attributes available per request

Having these attributes allows anyone to implement very different ways of protecting an API. Figure 6-1 shows two different levels (network, message) for these reasons:

- Network: Available attributes of this layer are generally available, independent of the application.

- Message: Available attributes of this layer usually depend on the type of application.

To visualize a protected API, but without showing snippets of code, see Figure 6-2. It is a screenshot of a drag-and-drop type programming[1] language and is well suited for a discussion of this topic.

---

[1]The CA API Gateway, www.ca.com/us/products/ca-api-gateway.html

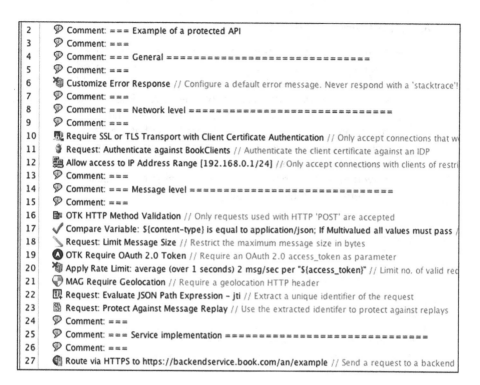

2	💬 Comment: === Example of a protected API	
3	💬 Comment: ===	
4	💬 Comment: === General ================================	
5	💬 Comment: ===	
6	🗐 Customize Error Response // Configure a default error message. Never respond with a 'stacktrace'!	
7	💬 Comment: ===	
8	💬 Comment: === Network level ============================	
9	💬 Comment: ===	
10	🔒 Require SSL or TLS Transport with Client Certificate Authentication // Only accept connections that w	
11	🖉 Request: Authenticate against BookClients // Authenticate the client certificate against an IDP	
12	🖥 Allow access to IP Address Range [192.168.0.1/24] // Only accept connections with clients of restri	
13	💬 Comment: ===	
14	💬 Comment: === Message level ===========================	
15	💬 Comment: ===	
16	🗐 OTK HTTP Method Validation // Only requests used with HTTP 'POST' are accepted	
17	✔ Compare Variable: ${content-type} is equal to application/json; If Multivalued all values must pass /	
18	✎ Request: Limit Message Size // Restrict the maximum message size in bytes	
19	Ⓐ OTK Require OAuth 2.0 Token // Require an OAuth 2.0 access_token as parameter	
20	🗐 Apply Rate Limit: average (over 1 seconds) 2 msg/sec per "${access_token}" // Limit no. of valid req	
21	🌐 MAG Require Geolocation // Require a geolocation HTTP header	
22	🔢 Request: Evaluate JSON Path Expression – jti // Extract a unique identifier of the request	
23	🖼 Request: Protect Against Message Replay // Use the extracted identifer to protect against replays	
24	💬 Comment: ===	
25	💬 Comment: === Service implementation ===================	
26	💬 Comment: ===	
27	🔷 Route via HTTPS to https://backendservice.book.com/an/example // Send a request to a backend	

Figure 6-2. *Screenshot of a protected API*

The screenshot can be interpreted like this:

- Numbers on the left are line numbers.

- Each line represents an "assertion." In Java, it would be a method; in JavaScript, it would be a function.

- Most lines have a right-hand side comment, which is displayed in light gray.

- Each line that starts with "Comment" represents, who would have guessed it, a comment.

- A request is received at the top and processed to the bottom. This means that each assertion is applied to the current request, just as in any other programming language.

Now that I have clarified how to read the screenshot, below are details on each step of that API. To summarize it, the implementation tries to filter out as many invalid requests as possible before calling the backend system on line 27.

Line 6: Default error message

- A template error message is specified. It is extremely important to handle potential errors, even errors based on bugs, within the implementation! An API should never expose an undefined error message. The worst error responses include details about failed database connections or server version details. Whatever may enable a hacker to manipulate the system cannot be exposed! Figure 6-3 is an example of an error I just received after clicking a button on a website, something no system should ever display.

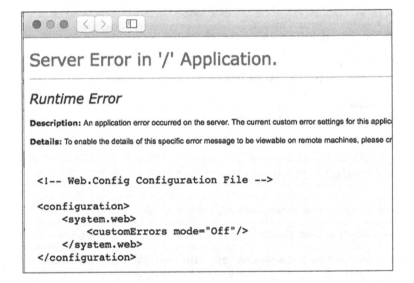

Figure 6-3. Error screen

- No matter which assertion after line 6 fails, only the specified error message will be returned as a response.

Line 10: Require TLS/SSL (network level)

- TLS/SSL is required to access this API. Any other attempt will fail. The API cannot be consumed.

- In this case, the requesting client needs to present its own X.509 Certificate[2]. This is also referenced as "mutual SSL" or "SSL with client authentication." Only a client that can present a certificate is able to consume this API.

---

[2]X.509, https://de.wikipedia.org/wiki/X.509

Line 11: **Authenticate the client (network level)**

- This line represents an IDP (identity provider). The client needs to be authenticated against this IDP using the provided X.509 certificate as its credential.

- Only authenticated clients are able to consume this API.

Line 12: **Limit valid IP addresses (network level)**

- The requesting client needs to have an IP address[3] that falls into a range of permitted IP addresses.

- This is a typical check for APIs that have restrictions on availability in regard to geolocations. For example, a gambling web site may restrict the usage of its APIs based on provinces due to laws that are in place. Restricting IP addresses is usually part of other geofencing[4] requirements.

- Limiting IP addresses should be used with caution if mobile devices are expected to support client applications. Mobile devices are carried around and change IP addresses potentially often. The devices may be at the edge of valid geolocations but would not be able to send valid requests due to an overlap of valid area and invalid IP address.

Line 16: **HTTP method (message level)**

- Only requests received via HTTP POST methods are accepted. Since this API also expects a message of a given type (see line 17) PUT could also be possible, but here not accepted.

Line 17: **Type of message (content-type, message level)**

- The request needs to match the message type application/json[5]. Especially in HTTP-heavy environments, different types are often found. On the other hand, a specific API most likely only supports one type. In this case, it's only type application/json.

- Only requests that contain a message of this type will be processed.

---

[3]IP address, https://en.wikipedia.org/wiki/IP_address
[4]Geofencing, https://en.wikipedia.org/wiki/Geo-fence
[5]Content-Type, https://en.wikipedia.org/wiki/Geo-fence

Line 18: Limit message size (message level)

- APIs are usually built to support well-defined types and formats of messages and with that the expected message size is known. This line limits the request to a maximum size in bytes. Anything larger is considered to be invalid.

Line 19: Require an OAuth 2.0 access_token (message level)

- The requesting client needs to present an OAuth access_token in order to consume this API.

- This access_token may not be expired but issued with certain permissions (scope). Keep in mind that scope only relates to the client, not the resource_owner!

- At this point, the API could also check if the resource_owner associated with the access_token is authorized to access it. This information cannot be derived from the access_token itself! What has to happen is an extra step. The resource_owner (username) has to be sent to an authorization service. This can be done via an API call or an LDAP lookup, depending on the system. In any case, this requires extensive discussions and good design!

Line 20: Rate limiting (message level)

- This API limits clients to consuming this API only twice per second. The provided access_token is used as an identifier.

- Rate limiting is sometimes controversial since it limits a client's performance. However, this API has to serve more than one client and it has a dependency on a backend service (line 27).

- When it comes to rate limiting, always remember that it's not about limiting clients but about *protecting any backend system* from failing!

Line 21: Require geolocation (message level)

- The request needs to provide an HTTP header named geolocation that contains latitude/ longitude. This information can be used to compare the location that is associated with the client's IP address, a second vector in the context of geofencing.

- Generally, the geolocation has to be translated into a real address, which can be done by using an external service.

- If the link below is copied into a browser, it will take you to downtown Vancouver. The bold numbers are longitude and latitude. This is how these values could be provided by a client:

```
https://www.google.com/maps/place/49°17'02.3%22N+123°07'
08.8%22W/@49.2839749,123.1196665,19z/data=!3m1!4b1!4m6!3
m5!1s0x0:0x0!7e2!8m2!3d49.2839741!4d-123.1191184
```

Lines 22/ 23: Protect against replay (message level)

- Line 22 extracts an identifier of the incoming message. Line 23 is using that identifier to protect against replays. The idea is to accept any message once only.

- Replay protection is required in cases where messages may change the state of a system. For example, submitting a transaction twice may not be a good idea since it will cause double bookings.

Line 27: Calling a backend

- Finally, after all those checks between line 2 and 23, a backend service is called. The backend request may contain details of the original incoming request.

- The API will return the response of this backend request to the original client.

To emphasize the need for API protection, let's assume the referenced backend service is hosted on a mainframe. Mainframe usages are charged by CPU cycles! As a service provider, you only want relevant requests to be forwarded to the mainframe. And even if there is no mainframe involved, your backend service may be hosted in serverless environments where charges are applied per request.

When looking at Figure 6-2, imagine a big funnel, wide open at the top and small at the bottom, ending at line 27. Whenever an API is built, it should reject as many requests as possible right at the top. To do this, here is a guideline to remember:

Catch invalid requests as early as possible!

It may sound obvious, but I have seen many implementations that did not follow this guideline. These implementations executed checks and validations that most likely *did not fail* first! The goal is the opposite! Otherwise, code will be executed, only to find out later that it wasn't necessary at all!

The guidelines above could be implemented this way:

1. Check for values that are most likely invalid, early.

2. Implement checks that are least expensive, early.

Figure 6-2 checks for the correct HTTP method and content-type very early on lines 16 and 17. These checks are very cheap, just simple string comparisons. It then checks for valid OAuth access_tokens on line 19 since this will fail often due to their expiration date. This is not the cheapest check but it's more likely to happen than violations against the replay protection on line 23. Replay protection is also not cheap, but in a distributed environment, it's more expensive than the access_token check.

API Error Handling

Error handling is not a famous topic as far as I can tell. Surprisingly I have not been in discussions on this topic often. It usually comes up only during panic-mode escalations when the operations team cannot find reasons for failing systems. In that moment, all involved team members are surprised about the absence of a meaningful error framework.

A product I designed used to generate error messages that were often wrong. It indicated an error that had happened but wasn't responsible for a failing request. Developers received an error message and investigated in a wrong direction. It was painful and I felt bad.

This experience caused a complete change of the product's architecture, which took quite a while. Today the produced error messages are correct, maintained in just one location, and easy to update. The work resulted in guidelines that I follow myself and suggest to customers. Now it is time to share those guidelines with a greater audience. Here they are:

1. **The API owner must be in control of error messages**. This sounds like a given but especially when choosing a middleware product, it should be evaluated if internal errors may be returned instead of ones created by the API owner/developer. That is not desired.

2. **APIs should return correct error messages.** This is another one that should be a given. However, if this is not the case, developers will be very confused.

3. **Error messages should not reveal sensitive information.** The error message should not expose implementation details such as stack traces. Error messages should be as general and as specific as possible at the same time. For example, returning *authentication*

failed due to invalid credentials is general but also specific enough. It would be wrong to return *authentication failed due to the incorrect password "xyz."*

4. **Error messages should be returned in an expected message format**. If the API consumes and produces JSON messages, error messages should also be returned in JSON.

5. **Error messages should be maintained in a single location**. This may be controversial and depends on the API development environment. But, if many APIs have to be managed, a system that has a central location for maintaining error messages may be used. Otherwise, if the error messages are formulated within those APIs directly, it may be difficult to change or fix them.

6. **The same errors should always cause the same error message.** If an API implements parameter validation and fails, the produced error message should be the same across all APIs that implement the same validation. This should be consistent for all types of errors.

7. **All possible error responses should be documented**. Do not let your API consumers guess what errors may occur. Document all possible errors that may be returned. This includes potential reasons for a failed request and also solutions for how this can be fixed. For example, if the error says *token is invalid*, you may want to document *The given access_token has expired. Repeat the request using a valid access_token.*

Typically, HTTP-based APIs return error messages with an HTTP status code of 400 and up.[6] This is helpful but may leave questions. For example, HTTP status 400 indicates that a client caused an error. However, there may be multiple reasons that could have caused the error. With no other indicator than the HTTP status code, it is difficult for the client to continue the workflow since it cannot decide what to do next.

To solve this problem, here are a few suggestions:

- Create a system that uses each HTTP status for one specific error case only.

- Create a system that has a well-defined short list of possible cases that create a specific HTTP status code.

---

[6]HTTP status codes, www.w3schools.com/tags/ref_httpmessages.asp

- Introduce a second level of status codes. They could be introduced as HTTP headers and would be application-specific. An example can be found within FAPI[7] (Financial API), which has proposed such a system.[8]

API Caching

API caching refers to a widely used technology, caching of data. In a world of APIs, caching is very important in the context of performance, meaning reduced response times and increased numbers of handled requests.

Caching, in general, tries to reduce the number of CPU or latency intensive processes with lightweight alternatives. Creating the alternative is done by keeping data in an easily accessible storage location. A typical example is the retrieval of datasets from a database (file based) and storing those datasets in an in-memory cache. The next request will not receive the dataset from the database but from the cache. There are different categories, different technologies, and different goals to be achieved. Most cases I have seen had two main requirements:

1. Reduce the number of database queries.

2. Reduce the number of API calls to external services.

At a first glance, caching sounds like the best invention since bread and butter. But, in reality, using caches successfully is anything but easy. The very big challenge with caching is the accuracy of the cached data. Even the simple example from above provokes the following question:

How is a dataset in a cache as accurate as in the database?

This question has to be asked over and over again and it has to be answered by the correct design of the API system. It has to be asked to avoid situations where a cache returns stale data. To explain this better, here is an example. A typical flow could work as shown in Figure 6-4.

---

[7]Financial API, http://openid.net/wg/fapi/

[8]FAPI error handling, https://bitbucket.org/openid/fapi/src/f1b3c95660dc e93404f2ff10aabb051b48ac718e/Financial_API_WD_004.md?at=master& fileviewer=file-view-default#markdown-header-7-api-errors

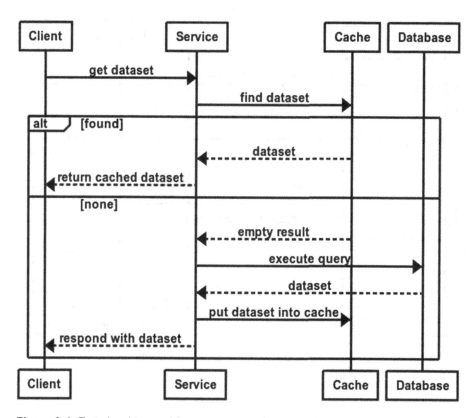

Figure 6-4. Typical caching workflow

If a dataset is found in the cache, it is returned. Otherwise, it will be retrieved from the main source (database) first and then copied into the cache. This process works as long as the cached dataset has an expiration date and if the cache is flushed if the content of the main source changes. In this example, an update of the dataset in the database should cause a flush of the dataset in the cache.

Unfortunately, Figure 6-4 supports none of the required features that are necessary for a successful caching system. It needs to be enhanced. The better version is displayed in Figure 6-5.

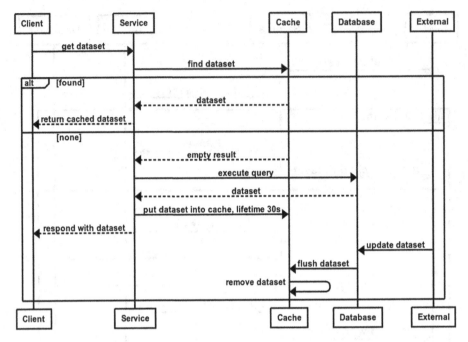

Figure 6-5. A slightly enhanced version of the simple caching system

Two enhancements:

1. The service adds a dataset to the cache and sets the lifetime to 30 seconds. This causes the service to retrieve the dataset from the database at least every 30 seconds.

2. The database flushes the cache after an update. This causes the service to retrieve the dataset from the database, even if it has not been updated.

Someone may say that a flushed cache after an update of the database is good enough. And it may be true, but it also prevents any invalid cached dataset being returned based on timing issues between "expired cache dataset lifetime" and "update database."

If you have ever implemented a caching or database solution, you may see something strange in Figure 6-4. The database got updated and afterwards notified the cache to flush a dataset. This is usually not supported. The question is, *Is that reality?* Yes and no: no for plain database systems and yes for API-based solutions. Here is a suggestion, which I call DataManager:

- To update or retrieve datasets, do not use connections to a caching or database system but use a DataManager.

- A DataManager controls access to data and updates or retrieves it from/to a database or caching solution or both.

- A DataManager provides APIs for all tasks.

Such a diagram looks like Figure 6-6.

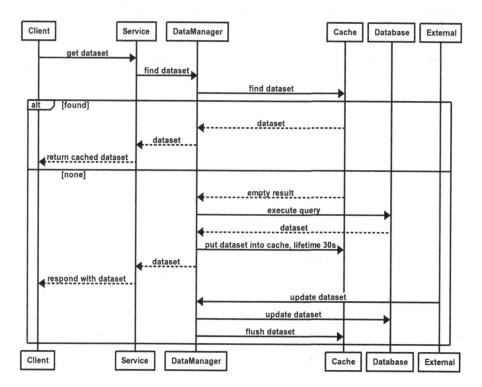

Figure 6-6. Enhanced flow using a DataManager

These are the main differences:

- Any communication to the storage layer (cache, database) is controlled via the DataManager.

- No component accesses the cache or database directly.

- The DataManager retrieves data either from the cache or the database and updates them appropriately.

DataManagers are implemented per use case and should support the current requirements only. Do not try to cover future cases that are not even expressed yet.

In this section, I only covered caching on a server. In a larger environment, caches may exist at multiple components, which complicates the system. Caches could be found within clients, external APIs, internal APIs, or database systems. I always think of small boxes that are chained to each other, something like Figure 6-7.

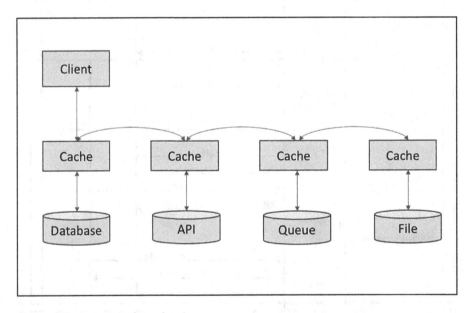

Figure 6-7. A view on chained caches

Figure 6-7 is not accurate, but it is a mind model I like to reference. It reminds me to ask which caches exist (or should exist) in conjunction with sources of different kinds, how they are configured, how they are refreshed, how they relate to each other, and what kind of cache they may be. This becomes even more important if the target system is a distributed environment.

Security vs. Performance

Caching improves API performance. That is a good thing. Nevertheless, there are limitations. Sometimes caching is not even an option.

- Caching is useful only if the same datasets are retrieved multiple times. If that is not the case, there is nothing to cache.

- Caching requires large amounts of memory. If memory is a constraint, caching may not be used or only for limited use cases.

- Caches keep datasets in memory. Some environments may not accept systems that keep sensitive information in memory. Caching is not an option here.

Despite these potential reasons for not introducing caching, there are certainly many good reasons for accepting, sometimes even requiring, the usage of caches. I would like to point out one specific case of caching that refers to cached authorization statements, in particular, caching in the context of OAuth.

OAuth token validations can be very expensive. They either require a token validation request to an authorization server, which introduces a dependency and latency, or they require JWT validation, which is CPU intensive. Caching, to me, sounds like an almost natural fit here, especially since OAuth token are used often in most cases. My thinking behind it is simple:

A token that is valid now is also valid 10 seconds from now!

The typical validation checks for required scope and expiration. In OAuth, an API caches the token validation result. To do so, a few things have to be considered beforehand:

- *Token validation cache lifetime* should be a fraction of the *token lifetime*, but they should have a fixed ratio to each other.
    - Short token lifetime → short cache lifetime and vice versa
    - Typical: token lifetime = 3600s → cache lifetime = 30s
- *Token validation cache lifetime influences the API performance.*
    - Short cache lifetime → bad performance

- *API performance* improves with longer *token lifetime.*
  - Short token lifetimes cause clients to request new tokens often, which requires a full authorization cycle.
- *API security* increases or decreases based on the configured lifetimes.
  - API security refers to the validity of the OAuth token validation result. It could happen that a cached but expired token can still be used, depending on the implementation!

The relationships are shown in Figure 6-8.

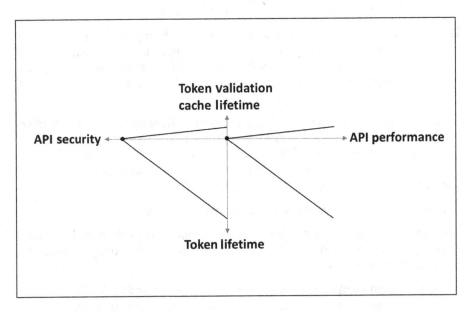

Figure 6-8. Attributes that influence API security

Figure 6-8 visualizes the conflict between API security and API performance. It also shows that the maximum cache lifetime should be in relation to the maximum token lifetime.

API Documentation

Chapter 4 covered API design and the topic of API documentation. Here I want to discuss a few important concepts. As explained earlier, documentation artifacts should be human and machine readable.

I am bringing up the machine-readable documentation again because that artifact should be as close to your APIs as possible. Specifically, it should be available through its own API! Many developers have the mind set of *Who reads documentation?* They believe they simply do not need it. But the majority, at least in my experience, of developers feel they have to search too long to find what they are looking for.

With that in mind, an API-driven system should make access to documentation as easy as sending a HTTP request to an API. For example, if a service is accessible through this API,

https://example.com/account

the documentation could be available at

https://example.com/**doc**/account

The usage can even be enhanced by providing different types of documentation that could be requested through simple query parameters:

- https://example.com/doc/account?**doctype =swagger**
- https://example.com/doc/account?**doctype=wadl**

It is difficult to make it easier than that!

The reason why the documentation URL should not be an extension of the service API (.../account/**doc** instead of .../**doc**/account) is based on the first part of this chapter that discussed API protection. Usually documentation should be publicly available whereas services are not. Services are implemented with mechanisms that restrict and limit accessibility, as discussed earlier.

If the documentation API is an extension (.../account/**doc**), the service API will have to support a flow that varies based on the URL path's ending! Technically that is not too challenging, but it influences the development process. Any update on the documentation would also be an update on the service API itself and would require a new test cycle. The service would need to implement logic such as this:

```
if (request.URL.path.endsWith("/doc"))
then (return documentation)
else (apply restrictions and process request);
```

This snippet may look simple but in larger systems it will happen sooner or later until the check for the doc fails and restrictions are bypassed, especially since some restrictions, such as `require SSL`, must be applied always and others, such as `require oauth access_token`, only to portions.

In comparison, having the documentation API separated from the service API allows an update at any given time. The worst thing that may happen is a mismatch between service implementation and documentation. That is annoying, but less annoying (and potentially catastrophic) than a broken service API!

To finish this topic up, other enhancements could also be supported. For example, the machine-readable documentation could be returned in a format that is human readable! The documentation API could support additional query parameters:

```
https://example.com/doc/account?doctype=swagger&format=html
```

The response would now be a (hopefully) beautiful HTML page suited for humans. In general, anything that makes it easier to provide the documentation is a step towards API adoption, which is one of the main goals for an API-based system!

Summary

This chapter gave an introduction to implementation details on securing APIs and preventing them from being consumed by non-authenticated or authorized entities. API error handling was introduced, as was API caching. The section on API documentation showed how easy access to documentation can increase the adoption of API-based systems.

API Gateways

In previous chapters, API gateways were introduced. Now it is time to look at them in detail. On a high level, these components are proxies that enable introspection of any message received and returned. They work on TCP level 3 – 5.[1] Figure 7-1 shows a view of the topology within a simple network that includes an API proxy (I'm using both terms, API gateway and API proxy, to emphasize that they are the same).

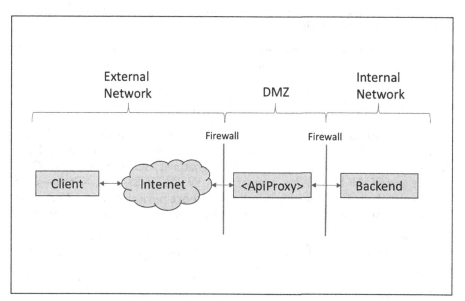

Figure 7-1. Typical network topology including an API gateway/API proxy

---

[1]Transmission Control Protocol, TCP, `https://tools.ietf.org/html/rfc793`

© CA 2018
S. Preibisch, *API Development*, https://doi.org/10.1007/978-1-4842-4140-0_7

Figure 7-1 displays the API gateway in between the external and the internal network, which is a very typical setup. It can look differently, too. It is not uncommon to find at least two API gateways. Many systems do not allow access to certain components from within the DMZ. For example, if data needs to be retrieved from a database, this database can only be accessed from within the internal network.

In those cases, one API gateway within the DMZ validates incoming messages by static rules only. These rules are configured once and do not need any additional information at runtime. After successful validation, that API gateway forwards the message to a second API gateway within the internal network. This one has access to all other components including databases and is able to complete a set of necessary validations.

Another trend that I have noticed during discussions with customers of large enterprises indicates that the distinction between the external and internal network has become less of a differentiator. These customers assume an attacker could be located anywhere. They are starting to place an API gateway as an Ingress gateway where traffic is received at the edge of their network and less powerful API gateways throughout different network sections. Each of them have very specific tasks and are usually responsible for securing a group of dedicated backend APIs (more on this design pattern in Chapter 8 about APIs and microservices).

The next sections are similar to each other, but they focus on different topics. Each one can be read on its own if that is preferred.

Why Do API Gateways Exist?

The first API gateways I noticed appeared in 2006. At that time, SOAP web services were still very new, and those messages could get very complex. XML schema validation, XML encryption, XML signatures, SOAP envelopes, SOAP headers and SOAP body, XML namespaces, WSDL, WSS, XSL, XPath—all of these technologies appeared in a relatively short period of time. And all of them had to be mastered in order to support a web service infrastructure.

If you remember these days, you will remember that it was not easy to get all these technologies right. Here is a short SOAP message for anyone who has not seen one:

```xml
<?xml version="1.0" encoding="UTF-8"?>
<soapenv:Envelope xmlns:soapenv="http://schemas.xmlsoap.org/soap/envelope/">
<soapenv:Body><soapenv:Fault>
<faultcode>soapenv:Server</faultcode>
<faultstring>Policy Falsified</faultstring>
<faultactor>https://example.com</faultactor>
<detail><gw:policyResult status="Service Not Found" xmlns:gw="http://
gateway.example.com/ws/policy/fault"/></detail>
</soapenv:Fault></soapenv:Body></soapenv:Envelope>
```

To process even a short message like this, many details need a developer's attention:

- Message structure
  - SOAP messages have an envelope and a body. The header is optional.
  - SOAP fault appears in error messages only.
- Two namespaces including aliases
  - soapenv:http://schemas.xmlsoap.org/soap/envelope/
  - gw:http://gateway.example.com/ws/policy/fault. This namespace is specific to this message
- Elements with no namespaces
  - faultcode, faultstring, faultactor, details
- Message encoding
  - UTF-8
- Elements and attributes

To access the value status, XPath is required. The expression looks like this:

```
/soapenv:Envelope/soapenv:Body/soapenv:Fault/detail/
gw:policyResult/@status
```

That is quite a selector for such a short message! It is not easy to build by anyone who is new to XML-related technologies. For this purpose, some API gateways provide easy-to-use graphical interfaces that allow users to create this XPath expression by simply selecting the element based on an example message.

Unfortunately, wherever it was required to expose business interfaces as SOAP web services, developers needed to support these technologies in all of their APIs. This required specific knowledge and had potential for mistakes, especially when it came to encryption, digital signatures, and SAML. From a business logic point of view, having to support these technologies was considered overhead since they were not really part of the API feature itself.

Similar to mobile applications today, there is always the effort of implementing the foundation of the app. Components that handle security, authentication, authorization, session management, all of that is not really the app, but still required. To help mobile developers, SDKs are available to take care of many of these technologies.

For SOAP web services, products have been made available to help API developers, similar to mobile SDKs to help app developers. The first products I worked with were the Layer 7 SecureSpan SOA Gateway (later the CA API Gateway)[2] and IBM DataPower.[3] The main goal was to take the burden off of developers by supporting all these XML-based technologies in an easily accessible way. Developers could then concentrate on their API business logic and let the API gateways handle all the complicated, non-business API logic separately.

A typical scenario, which I have worked on myself, was the following.

A medical report would be sent to the health insurance company. The report would be signed and partially encrypted. In addition, the report would be sent via TLS with client authentication.

The API gateway would validate the SSL session, the digital signature, would check for rate limits and messages size, and it would do XML schema validation. It would take care of validating the complete message. Decrypting the message would be an option, depending on the use case. Developers of backend business APIs could now expect to handle validated messages only! For example, the signature validation would not be necessary since it was already done!

Nowadays these SOAP web services may still be running but new SOAP web services rarely appear. Instead, RESTful API interfaces have taken over. Although message structures may not be as complex anymore, the need for introspection still exists. The complex message structure has been replaced by having to support multiple parameters including optional ones, explicit HTTP method validations, and different types of payloads. Requirements such as rate limits and message size validations have not changed. In addition, new protocols such as OAuth and OpenID Connect have been created and need to be handled, too.

What Are API Gateways Used For?

A few features have been mentioned, but here I would like to share typical use cases that I have seen over the years. It is not easy to answer question because API gateways are usable in very versatile ways. To start off, here is an overview of the technological categories in which API gateways are often used:

1. Access control (i.e. who can access)

2. Network-level security (i.e. use of TLS)

---

[2]CA API Gateway, www.ca.com/us/products/ca-api-gateway.html
[3]IBM DataPower, www.ibm.com/ca-en/marketplace/datapower-gateway

3. Message security (i.e. message encryption)

4. Message validation and transformation (i.e. from JSON to XML)

5. Message routing (i.e. forwarding messages via HTTP)

6. API availability (i.e. accessible during certain hours)

7. Logging

8. Threat protection (i.e. protecting against SQL injection)

9. Support for messaging (i.e. HTTP to MQTT)

10. Support for accessing data sources (i.e. accessing databases)

It is a long list and it's not even complete. Other categories can be found, but they are more like "you can but you should not necessarily do this or that using an API gateway." As mentioned, on a high level it is all about externalizing non-business, API-related features in the API gateway. What that means in detail is described best by an example.

Let's say a business API has to validate and persist incoming paystubs. The requests must be sent by authorized clients who are identified by an OAuth access_token. The API must apply validations to assure reliability and security. Once the request has been validated, the API must associate the given paystub with a user and persist it. All actions must be logged for historical and compliance reasons.

However, the API developer needs to take care of all of these steps:

1. Error handling

2. SSL/TLS

3. OAuth with SCOPE paystub

4. Authentication

5. Authorization

6. Rate limit

7. Replay attack protection

8. Message size validation

9. SQL injection protection

10. Validate and persist paystub

As you can see, 9 out of 10 requirements are not directly related to the actual feature. A developer will spend a lot of time implementing those 9 requirements before he or she gets to number 10. When I think about implementation efforts for a single API like this, I have two different development modes in my mind:

1. Preparation → API infrastructure

   a. Effort spent to build some kind of foundation including requirements 1 - 9

2. Implementation → API business logic

   a. Effort spent implementing the actual, required logic for requirement 10

I visualize it as shown in Figure 7-2.

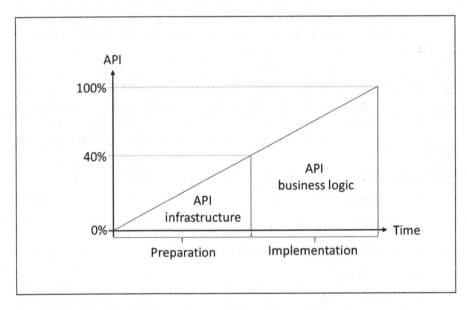

Figure 7-2. Effort for API infrastructure and API business logic

The percentage may not match in all cases, but it is roughly what I have seen in real-life scenarios. The point is, everything that is not part of the core feature of an API is part of its infrastructure. If you multiply this by the number of APIs, it can be imagined that many resources are used only to get to a point where the business implementation can be started.

The goal of having an API gateway is to externalize these tasks. With an API gateway, those 9 requirements can be implemented in front of the business API, done by a different developer team. And, even if it is the same team, the API gateway provides features that support the developers to get ahead fast. The API gateway not only speeds up implementations, it also eases the operation of services! Internal standards can be applied, logging can be aligned, and API protection can be aligned—all of this due to having one single component that "sees" all traffic.

After all, the business API only receives requests that have been validated. This also reduces the required processing power for them. Figure 7-3 displays this.

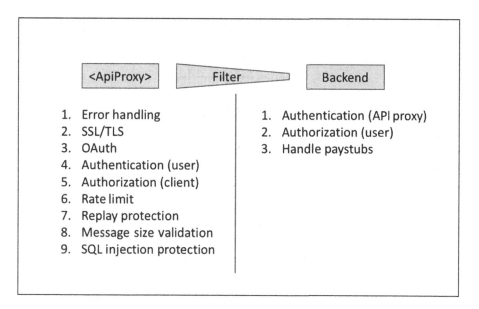

Figure 7-3. Implementing requirements, API proxy vs. backend

The API gateway takes care of most requirements and filters incoming requests to only forward valid messages to the backend. Steps 1 and 2 on the backend side are additional required steps. They are to assure that requests were received by the API proxy and that the user is the one associated with the paystub. After that, the backend can handle its paystub feature.

If you now ask why the user can't be authorized by the API proxy, the answer is quite simple: API gateways should not implement business-relevant validations! Only the business API itself should do that. Otherwise, a lot of context needs to be made available to the API gateway and that raises privacy concerns and potential replication challenges.

In many cases, the requirements in front of different business APIs will be the same, or at least similar. Knowing this opens the door for tremendous simplifications. Ideally it becomes so simple that a developer could be placed in front of a website and simply fill out a dialog with check boxes and input fields. A click on a "Deploy service" button will create a new API on the API proxy and all these requirements will be implemented. Simple as that!

I would like to share a prototype that I have worked on. This is the scenario.

A backend API is exposed via an API gateway. The API gateway must filter the incoming request, forward it to a backend, and inspect responses. If the responses are valid, they are returned to the requesting client. The web UI of the prototype looks similar to the one shown in Figure 7-4.

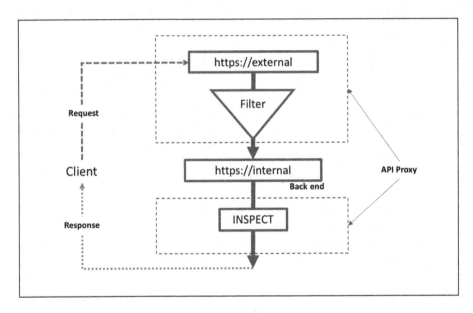

Figure 7-4. Prototype of a API proxy API builder

Each box represents a piece of required configuration for creating an API: the external URL (https://external), filter (RateLimit, Content-Type check), the backend URL (https://internal) that implements the business logic, and the response inspection (content inspection of the backend response) back to the requesting client. The web UI includes a few dialogs (Figure 7-5) that enable a developer to provide required values.

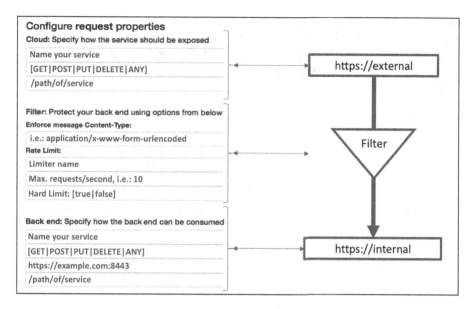

Figure 7-5. Dialog for providing required values for generating a proxy API

At the end a "Deploy service" button generates a deployment descriptor that goes into a version control system and is used to generate code for different API proxy target systems. Since the code for the API proxy is generated, no errors are possible. Each API follows best practices, include error handling and generating comments so that readers of the implementation will know what it does.

It is hopefully obvious that anyone could fill out these dialogs. No hardcore technology knowledge is needed. The best part about all of this is the fact that none of this influences the business API. It can be developed without knowing anything about the API proxy implementation. The contract between those two would be an API definition such as the Swagger document discussed previously.

Mocking APIs

I would like to share one of those use cases that are not always obvious. API gateways are great to "mock" services. If a client must be built to consume a backend API that has not yet been realized, testing tools can be used. However, another alternative is to use the API gateway that will later expose the proxy API. Until the backend API is completed, the proxy API can be built to take incoming requests and return success and error responses. Where Figure 7-5 shows a dialog to configure the backend API URL, it can simply be set to something like `http://localhost/fake`. The implementation would do nothing else than return a `HTTP status 200, fake` response message. This also speeds up the whole development process. To give an impression how easy this can be, Figure 7-6 displays a screenshot of such a fake API, implemented on CA API gateway.

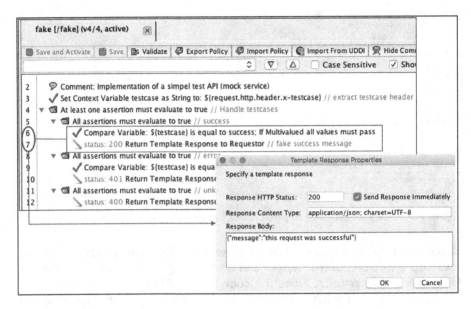

Figure 7-6. Implementation of a fake API for testing purposes (mock service)

A client passes in an HTTP header (line number 3) named `x-testcase`, which sets a variable named `testcase`. Further down the API takes the appropriate action. For a success message, it will return what is shown in the lower right dialog.

Many cases can be handled. It can also be done based on other incoming parameters or request payloads. Ideally the API gateway will require request messages and return responses that also match the Swagger API definition. With that, only the content would be fake, but message formats and structures could already be verified!

Another powerful feature is the capability of simulating failing backend systems, added latency, connection breakdowns—all the cases no one would like to see in a production system, but still need to handle!

Why Is It Important to Leverage API Gateways?

The first reason that comes to my mind for why it is important to leverage an API gateway is decoupling. An API gateway decouples more than one may think:

1. External network from internal network

2. External API interface from internal API interface

3. External URL from internal URL

4. External network topology from internal network topology

5. External API version from internal API version

The second reason is the separation of concerns:

1. The API gateway can be managed by a different team than the backend API team.

2. Teams such as operations (DevOps) or security can specify their own requirements without influencing the business API.

3. The separation of features per API. For example, the API gateway could expose a JSON-based API and translate that to an XML interface for the backend API. The API gateway can also translate between different protocols.

Another main reason is integration and scaling:

1. API gateways can connect to other components to prepare the request to the backend API.

2. API gateways can be scaled independently of backend APIs.

Other noticeable reasons, from a more general viewpoint, are the following:

1. Termination of TLS/ SSL connections

2. Service orchestration. One exposed API could leverage multiple other APIs internally. A response of a simple / overview API could be the result of five or more API calls, managed and implemented by the gateway.

3. Caching, to reduce the load of messages being send to the backend system

All these reasons enable different teams to work on features at the same time, each one on its own component. Let's have a closer look into each one.

Decoupling

Figure 7-7 gives an idea how attributes in regard to decoupling could be implemented and/ or supported.

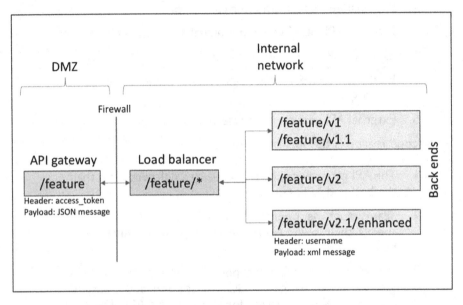

Figure 7-7. Decoupling between the API gateway and backend API

The API gateway is located within the DMZ and receives requests from external clients. The requests include an OAuth access_token and a JSON payload. The API gateway will validate the access_token and retrieve the associated username. In addition, it will inspect the payload. Depending on that, it is able to evaluate which backend API of which version should handle this message (this is also called content-based routing). Since the backend API requires an XML payload, the API gateway transforms the JSON payload into that.

The API gateway creates a request for the target backend API and includes the username as an HTTP header in addition to the XML payload. The load balancer in between the API gateway and the backend APIs serves one IP address, which resolves to the matching backend API by examining the requests URL path. Each target backend receives and processes the request that matches exactly their interface.

This setup provides the flexibility for the backend API developers to develop and test new versions whenever they feel like it. Once the backend API is ready for production, the load balancer can be updated to route to the new backend API if required. Lastly, the API gateways logic to inspect the payload gets updated. That enables it to include the new backend API as a target location. The API gateway can also be prepared earlier in the development process but either ignores requests that are received with a newer payload or simply forwards them to an older version. Many possibilities appear once this setup has been established.

Separation of Concerns

Figure 7-7 shows several components: the API gateway, a firewall, a load balancer, and multiple backend servers. What appears to be a complex setup at a first glance is very much required. The backend APIs may be maintained by different teams that are specialists in a particular area. At the same time, network administrators can update the load balancer with configurations as necessary. The API gateway can handle requirements that are not directly business API-relevant but reduce complexity in that area.

Often, components in the DMZ require special audits due to the nature of the DMZ. Everything in the DMZ is exposed to the Internet and is therefore a potential target for attacks. The security team can apply strong measures to reduce risks. This does not apply to the backend APIs since they are not located in the DMZ and message inspections are done in the DMZ. The risk of receiving an invalid message is very much reduced.

Although the separation is very useful, it also requires well documented interfaces. If one component goes down, a procedure to identify it quickly is needed. A useful trick to trace messages is to include a requestID that is supported practically everywhere. As soon as a request is received, a requestID should be created and included in all subsequent calls and back again. If this value is logged, it can be searched for it and the failing component can be identified, sometimes even by not finding the value for component xyz in the logs!

Integration and Scaling

Integration is a strong argument for the existence of API gateways. As an architect, I work with customers who have questions regarding this topic often! Typical integrations include custom IDPs (Active Directory, Oracle Access Manager, CA SSO, Open LDAP), different databases (MySQL, Oracle, Cassandra), FTP servers, email servers, mobile notifications—almost anything that is available. Even integrations with mainframes! Figure 7-8 gives an overview.

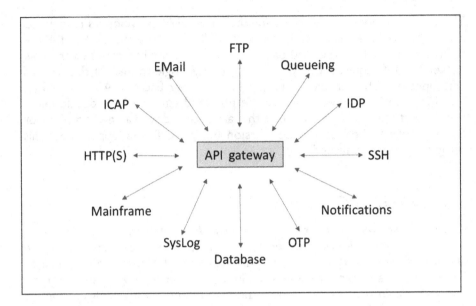

Figure 7-8. Typical integrations for API gateways

The beauty is that API gateways already support the technology to integrate with each of these systems. They only require configurations (exceptions exist). The backend API developer does not need to include a single line of code to support these integrations. Having these possibilities enables new use cases also. A request could be received via an email, checked for viruses using ICAP, and afterwards forwarded to a backend API. If this had to be handled by the backend itself, it could require skill sets that may not exist in teams.

■ **Note** Because of these integration capabilities, API gateways are sometimes also referred to as lightweight ESBs.[4] ESBs receive a request and processes it through many different channels until the message is finally sent to the main recipient.

Scaling is another big and important topic. Scaling may be required to serve a higher load from the external network but sometimes also into the internal network. A combination of both is certainly also possible. However, scaling is nothing that can be handled by any component itself. The network topology must be prepared for it. Adding a new API gateway or backend API is not an easy task and requires the correct setup beforehand. Needless to say, this is something that is necessary, no matter what component has to be scaled.

---

[4]ESB, enterprise service bus, https://en.wikipedia.org/wiki/Enterprise_service_bus

If the backend needs scaling, it can be done independently of the API gateway. Session stickiness between the API gateway and a particular backend API may be required but that can be handled. Scaling in that direction can also include rate limiting per backend API. The exposed API on the gateway can be configured to prevent the backend API from failing or getting overloaded.

Caching is also an interesting capability. Often, APIs return the same result, for example, configurations. In those cases, an API gateway could cache these types of responses for a specified amount of time to reduce the overall load to backend services and the overall latency.

In the other direction, looking into the external network, the API gateway itself may need to scale. In that case, it needs to be located behind a load balancer itself, and more nodes can be included. If scaling has not been a topic for anyone reading this section, Figure 7-9 illustrates what it means.

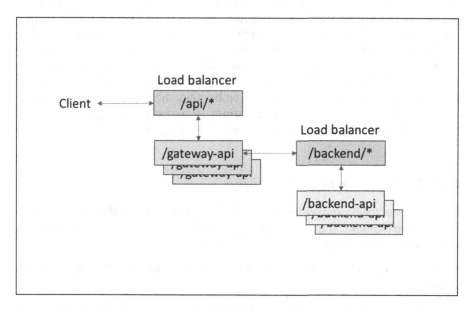

Figure 7-9. Scaling API gateways and backend APIs

Figure 7-9 contains multiple API gateways and backend APIs. It should illustrate the idea that components are created based on demand. Since they are all interconnected with each other in one way or the other, a well-planned strategy for scaling is required. A client will always send requests to the same address, but this request may be handled by different servers. This scenario needs to be supported! Having stateless components with no sessions is helpful but not always possible.

Having unique feature sets and playing such a vital role, API gateways are also great for auditing and logging. If all requests are processed by an API gateway, the API gateway is able to log and audit all messages if desired! This comes at a cost of decreased performance, but it may be valid for some environments. Turning on and off auditing and logging for certain time frames or during escalations is also possible.

Let's consider a case where employees use an enterprise app. However, this app sometimes fails for some users. In addition, due to their roles, the app may access an API on backend XXX and sometimes on backend ZZZ. If logging only exists on the backend APIs, it could be challenging to discover what is going wrong. Having the API gateway in-between allows logging of usernames, request times, target backend APIs, backend API response errors, latency between APIs—all in a central location no matter what the target API may be.

If you feel that logging and auditing causes concerns in regard to privacy or access control nightmares, there is good news. API gateways (at least some) include role-based access. It is possible to limit who can do what and who can see what based on user roles or other attributes. This not only includes access to log files or audits; this also includes access to deployed APIs. This can also be used to simplify the case where API gateways are shared between different teams. Depending on team membership, these developers may only have access to reading API implementations or audits or configurations. Fine granular controls are available and should be leveraged.

API Gateway Alternatives

As an architect who has worked with API gateways since 2006, I usually say, *There is no alternative. You need to have it!* Needless to say, this is too easy as an acceptable answer. Of course alternatives exist!

Here is a list of typical ones that come up when customers explain their current situation:

- **Home-grown**: Often, customers work with a home-grown solution. These systems usually start off as a small project to address exactly one requirement. Over time, more features are added as the need comes up. However, a typical conversation starts like this: *We have this home-grown system that we need to replace. We do not have anyone left who is able to maintain it anymore!* The other conversation sounds like this: *We would like to introduce an API gateway but many of our systems depend on our home-grown system. Your API gateway needs to integrate the home-grown token format until we have moved all systems* *off of it!* Don't get me wrong: home-grown systems are not generally bad ideas. But, as it happens, these systems are often not treated as a product and therefore the development does not follow best practices for product development lifecycles. Lack of documentation, lack of testing, lack of knowledge-sharing are some of the issues. The investment into existing products may be avoided. But if the home-grown system is not treated as a product right from the beginning, it will be more cost-intensive in the long run. This alternative usually grows organically. A developer has this cool idea and promises that he can implement this one single feature easily by himself. Since it worked out, he is asked to implement another feature. One after one, and suddenly it's a complete server that runs well, at least, as long as this one developer is around.

- **WAF[5] and security per REST API**: This option is found where environments serve pure REST APIs (i.e. JSON or XML payloads) and web content (i.e. HTML). Generally, environments that have started with web content only (web applications) leverage a WAF. Over time, when systems began to introduce REST services, the limitations of WAFs were compensated by adding features directly into each new REST API. Identified redundancies of common code was externalized and put into libraries or SDKs. For example, within a PHP-based ecosystem, REST APIs would use the same includes to handle rate limiting, message size validation, and other tasks. At some point in time, developers will have the desire to completely externalize these tasks into something like an API gateway or a WAF extension. And this ends up in a home-grown system again!

- **Per API solution**: Rare, but also seen, are systems where each API takes care of its own security in all aspects. Teams that maintain an API, or a group of APIs, implement the business logic and additionally anything else that is needed for securing them. Knowledge may be shared with other teams, but the main mindset follows the idea of *it has to work for us*. For example, a system that has multiple web sites or REST APIs that handle online payment. Or, at least, the collection of payment details in order to forward these to payment card processing

---

[5]WAF, web application firewall, https://en.wikipedia.org/wiki/Web_application_firewall

providers. How this collection of data is implemented or secured or displayed to users may be different per web site with no alignment between teams! As long as security reviews do not identify potential vulnerabilities and as long as the specific process is successful, any attempt for refactoring code is neglected. For this approach to be successful, the same requirements apply as they do for the home-grown use case.

A drawback of not having a dedicated component to handle incoming and outgoing traffic is the distribution of data. It is very difficult to apply company-wide, or at least business unit-wide, guidelines for securing and auditing APIs. Different teams have to be convinced of the usefulness and encouraged to follow these guidelines. Even small things like auditing become challenging since most teams have their own rules for auditing what, when, and how. If teams feel that adhering to these guidelines requires extra effort, they will ignore them as long as possible!

Nevertheless, I have seen one example where customers built a well-working system themselves. It was built from the ground up. The reason for its success was the fact that a team was formed and treated as a product development team. Requirements were collected, the scope of the project was well defined, timelines were specified, and releases were made available often to collect feedback from other employees. In addition, the system was well documented.

Summary

API gateways (API proxies) play a vital role in any environment that exposes RESTful APIs. API gateways are located so that all incoming and outgoing traffic can be inspected by them. Applying security rules, implementing logging requirements, enabling reviewers—all of this is supported. The burden of implementing non-functional requirements in regard to a business API is taken of the developers' plates. Each team can concentrate on its own strengths. Alternatives do exist, but they often end up being a maintenance nightmare and difficult to manage.

APIs and Microservices

After discussing API design and implementation details, it is now time to discuss how APIs and microservice architecture fit together. This topic has been popular for quite some time and enterprises have started to move towards this design pattern. The content of this chapter is based on questions and discussions with customers. Martin Fowler's article "Microservices" is available for anyone who wants to learn more about microservice architecture[1] in general.

A microservice architecture refers to a design pattern that emphasizes the idea of having APIs be self-contained and serve one purpose only. Each API should be deployable through an automated process. An application may use multiple APIs that are grouped by business purpose. A microservice architecture should create a system that is highly fault tolerant, scalable, deployable, maintainable, and allows you to add and remove single APIs.

What Is the Difference Between APIs and Microservices?

At a first glance, APIs and microservices ("services" for short) are the same thing with different names. Both receive requests and produce expected responses. The external views on APIs and services do not give any hint to

---

[1]Martin Fowler, "Microservices," https://martinfowler.com/articles/microservices.html

© CA 2018
S. Preibisch, *API Development*, https://doi.org/10.1007/978-1-4842-4140-0_8

what they are. The differences are their internals, in regard to implementation details, deployment model, dependencies, and the scope of features they serve. In this chapter, I will refer to APIs as the old way of doing things and microservices (or services) as the new way of doing things.

APIs may be implemented on a server that hosts many other non-related APIs too. APIs receive requests and handle them but may also send requests to other APIs to complete their tasks. Unfortunately, when hosted on the same server, some APIs retrieve other API resources directly, for example, by connecting to an API's database. This type of intercommunication is a recipe for expensive maintenance costs in all possible ways. This pattern is not uncommon and has caused many escalations and reduced software upgrades to rare events.

Microservices are built to serve one purpose only. Services that have different business purposes are not colocated on the same server. Services only communicate with other components via documented and provided interfaces.

Figure 8-1 displays the difference between APIs and services.

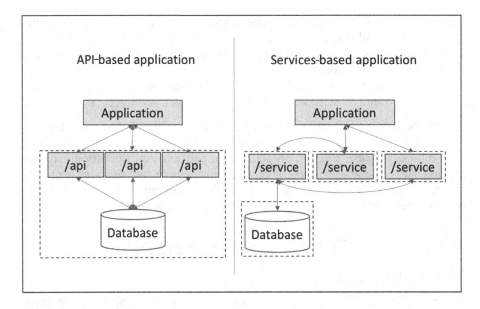

Figure 8-1. High-level view of API and services-based applications

In Figure 8-1 the application on the right side is based on a services architecture. The application leverages services but they don't run on their own servers. An update of one service does not influence the other ones. In addition, one service is dedicated to communicating with the database and through it other services access the database. Each service can be scaled horizontally, independent of others.

The application on the left side is based on an architecture where a single server provides practically all features. In addition, all APIs access the database directly. Updating or replacing one of those APIs or the database schema is difficult. The regression test effort may be huge, depending on the behavior of the APIs. This is a scenario where it may take weeks or even months before an upgrade can be deployed. This is not unusual; I have seen it in customer environments. Having this type of architecture prevents systems from being updated regularly, which means that new features and security updates cannot be made available when they should be.

I recently attended a public event in Vancouver, hosted by a social platform, and the message was, *Our website gets updated up to three times per day, our mobile app once a week. It is very unlikely that two attendees here have the same version of our app!'* That was pretty impressive.

It is difficult to top that dynamic environment. In spite of knowing about this possibility, it should not be the first goal when coming from a *twice per year* upgrade rhythm. Having multiple servers, multiple databases, each component communicating with others, everything tangled together is a tough situation. Being able to update such a system at least once per month is probably a big step ahead already.

The question is, *How can we get from an API-based architecture to a services-based architecture with independent services everywhere?*

The first step is to find out what exists. Often not even the current state is known. If developers are asked, *What does this API do?*, the answer may be *Not sure, but it seems to work!'* Knowing that these kinds of answers will be given, you should ask different development teams to create dependency and entity diagrams to explain how their individual systems work. After collecting and tying together different diagrams, you can get a larger picture and the existing system will start to get transparent, which is one of the most crucial requirements for this task.

After the system has been documented, including communication channels between different entities, a small piece should be identified, ideally a piece of the system that is serving one business purpose only. This should be the Guinea pig for the transformation from a monolithic to a services-based application.

Developers should move this service onto its own server. For example, if it is a Java application, it could be deployed into an Apache Tomcat[2] or JBoss server.[3] As soon as these services are deployable and locally tested, they should be taken into a QA environment where test clients can verify their function. Once that is successful, clients who have been consuming the original service

---

[2]Apache Tomcat, http://tomcat.apache.org
[3]JBoss, www.jboss.org

should switch to the new one. Step by step this service can be promoted to different environments. If this promotion is a manual task, this is the right time to start turning it into an automated process, even if it is only a bunch of scripts. It is important to get started!

■ **Note**   I sometimes hear people say that *automation is not possible*. This is usually not true. Instead, it has not been done before, it is difficult, and it requires changes in processes. No matter what, enabling automation must be a focus in the development, testing, and deployment process!

With some effort, including the automation, developers should find themselves in a situation where a check-in into a version control system (VCS)[4] is all it takes to get a new version of a service deployed, or at least built. Getting this done in a test and/or development environment is the first step. It will take some time to figure out the details of how to do (or not to do) things, but it is a good feeling when a test server suddenly hosts an updated version of code with no manual effort. It also teaches everyone how not to break services interfaces without notifying anyone else because other developers, whose services consume these ones, will complain immediately!

Visualized, the process could look like Figure 8-2.

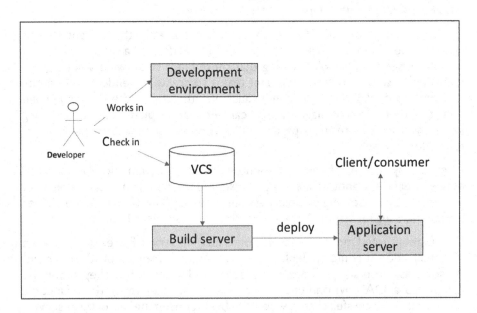

Figure 8-2. High level and simplified lifecycle of service development

---

[4]VCS, version control system, example Git: https://git-scm.com/book/en/v2/ Getting-Started-About-Version-Control

Figure 8-2 indicates that a developer (or a group of developers) keeps her work within a development environment. She goes through all tasks that are needed to get the system up and running. Once she is done, she checks her code into the VCS. When this happens, a build server kicks off and executes automated tests, configures the services, and creates artifacts as needed. When this step successfully ends, the build server deploys the service into the target environment's application server. This server instantiates the artifacts and the updated service becomes available.

Figure 8-2 is very simple, but in the end, it is always the same process, sometimes including a few more steps than shown but basically like that. Depending on the environment, the application server may host more than a single or logical group of services. Due to resource limitations this may not be avoidable, but, regardless, services should not have implicit dependencies to each other.

The automated process enables teams to redeploy services often. A bug was found, it got fixed (and nothing else), tested, checked in, and deployed. Considering my own experience, any manual task that can be eliminated is a step towards automated deployability. Updates do not need to be scheduled over months; they may not be scheduled at all! As long as interfaces do not change, clients will not need to be updated and can continue even with the latest service.

Note Automated tests have very little value if a failing test raises the question *Was it the test or the implementation that caused the failure?* This question indicates missing trust in the test system and, with that, in the quality of the tested product itself!

The last few paragraphs got a little mixed up with the next section. Nevertheless, if the process of extracting services out of monolithic applications had its first small success stories, it becomes easier to follow the microservices pattern.

What to Know When Supporting a Microservice Infrastructure

Having the term "infrastructure" in this section's title should indicate that there is more to microservices than just modifying the implementation. As mentioned in the previous chapter, it should be possible to automate the deployment of services. This requires a CI/CD[5] pipeline that avoids as many manual tasks as possible. This is not only necessary to enable automation but also because the team members who will deploy the software are not part of the group of software developers.

---

[5]CI/ CD = continuous integration, continuous deployment

To support a good working CI/CD pipeline, other groups than only developers are required. Network infrastructure experts, security experts, support, operations—all these groups are needed. Over the last two or three years the term DevOps[6] was introduced and now refers to the whole process. DevOps emphasizes the fact that development and operations are working hand in hand (specifically development, QA, and operations). Each involved group between development and deployment has its own tasks, but at the same time the needs of other groups are respected.

If you are currently not following the DevOps principle, you may wonder what the difference to your current process may be. Here are a few thoughts of mine, based on real life experiences:

- Your developers implement, test, document, and release software into production environments all by themselves.

- QA is testing software manually.

- Network administrators accompany developers to open up server rooms and provide access to servers so that these developers can manually deploy new versions of software straight into production.

- The database administrator is on stand-by during an upgrade to rescue failed attempts and suggest default values for database configurations.

- You do have operations teams who have received instructions for manual software installations. The instructions assume deep knowledge of the software, which does not exist. After 5.5 hours of following instructions, the process is rolled back due to some undocumented and missing parameters (the procedure to roll back is not documented, so operations must figure it out on the fly).

- QA has never tested the software in a production-like system (the development environment is the same as production anyways ...).

- You had to postpone a release due to a sick developer whose knowledge is required during an upgrade.

- Systems have to be taken offline to run the upgrade. SLAs state very clearly how long this may take, and additional periods will result in costly penalties. To reduce the chance of having to pay those penalties, the number of releases is limited to two per year.

---

[6]DevOps, Development and Operations, www.atlassian.com/devops

If all of the above, or at least a few of them, are true for your current environment, it is a strong indicator that some work lies ahead of you. The work is not only referring to implementations, but in changing the mindsets of teams. Current processes have to change!

In order to enhance existing processes, they have to be broken apart. Once that is done, each process needs to have an owner. Owners are responsible for everything that falls into their scope and they have to be very clear about the requirements that need to be successful. Each team has to assume that others are experts in their own processes only. Without that, upgrades or installations will often fail. Let's look at this by example:

> **Developer**: *I have written all 15 steps you need to follow to install the upgrade. Have a good evening. See you on Monday!*

> **Operations**: *Ok, I will follow them tonight during the maintenance window.*

The instructions say *Open the installations menu and provide the default username*. Guess what? Operations will already be stuck. They do not know how to open the installations menu nor are they aware of the default username! This little example is not fake. I witnessed it (not saying who I was in that scenario)!

There were a few mistakes made:

1. The developer assumed that operations knew how to open the installation menu.

2. The developer assumed that operations knew the default username.

3. Operations did not go through the instructions when the developer was still around.

In larger scenarios there are almost endless possibilities for failure! For that reason, development and operations need to work close together. For example, after the above situation, operations shared with the developer that they are maintaining more than 30 systems at the same time. It is impossible for them to be experts on all systems and to know the default username for each one of them.

To get to a working CI/CD pipeline, teams have to discuss all steps of the deployment process in detail. Each team has to understand others and be very clear on what they can handle and what they can't. Once that has been clarified, the same instructions from above may look like this:

Developer: *I have written all 15 steps you need to take to install the upgrade. I also included a script that executes steps 1-6 and 9-11 if you prefer that. Usernames, passwords, locations for menus are all documented. I will be home later, but I have left my phone number for the worst-case scenario.*

Operations: *Let me just check the instructions …. Ok, I got it, Looks good. I will do a dry run right now and give you a call if something is missing. I will use the scripts to reduce the chance of errors caused between the screen and the keyboard. Thanks!*

Runbooks

The written instructions are also called runbooks. Runbooks should have straightforward instructions but also cover anything that may happen outside the happy-path deployment process (this may even be the most important content, recovering from errors). A good runbook is created by team work! Operations must be able to install new systems or upgrade existing systems just by following the runbook instructions.

Creating the runbook is an iterative process. It goes back and forth between different teams, mainly the ones shown in Figure 8-3.

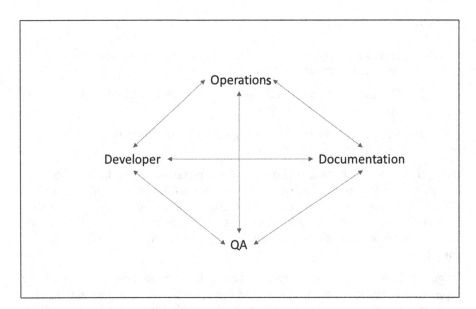

Figure 8-3. Participants in creating a runbook

The shown groups may vary, but Figure 8-3 should be more or less accurate for environments that own the complete process.

Developers implement and build software and create a runbook based on their current deployment experiences. This draft is reviewed by *operations* and used in production-like environments. Their review results in a list of updates and a set of questions and recommendations. *Documentation* reviews the instructions and applies the feedback. In between, *QA* verifies that no steps for validating the software's function are missing. This iterative process ends with a runbook that enables operations to install or upgrade systems with confidence.

■ **Note**   The *documentation* team is not always mentioned in the context of creating a runbook. Nevertheless, technical writers are the ones who can help formulate instructions to be understood in the target language. Developers and QA members often work in environments that use languages other than their native ones. For example, our documentation team turns my German-English into English frequently.

An accepted runbook is the first step towards a working DevOps process. Having this runbook points out that the team understands and respects everyone's needs. Once this has been established, the next step waits.

Automating the Runbook!

Yes, automation is the overall goal for the process. Only automated processes permit frequent service deployments with low risk of failures. Where the first runbook is good for deployments that happen once in a while or environments with just a few services, the automated runbook is a prerequisite for enterprise-level systems with hundreds of services. To me, this became very obvious when I had lunch with a previous colleague who said, *Sascha, I develop the code, I write the unit test, I commit it. That's it! After a few days, my code runs in production and I have no clue how it got there!'* She did know that her code was tested in an automated QA pipeline and reviewed at some point. But the interesting part for me was that developers did not need to know the details of the deployment pipeline (the automated runbook).

Getting to that stage of automation is a challenge. However, after multiple runbook iterations and better understanding of *what can go wrong and how can it be fixed*, all teams understand how essential it is to remove manual tasks of the deployment process. Figure 8-4 is the generally accepted view of required CI/CD steps.

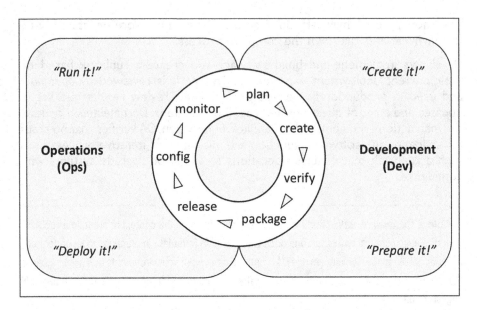

Figure 8-4. Steps of a CI/CD pipeline

Figure 8-4 lists the steps that are considered part of the CI/CD pipeline. It is an endless, ever-repeating circle. The left half contains tasks and asks for operations (Ops) and the right half the tasks and asks for development (Dev), which also includes QA. This image also indicates the hand-off from Dev to Ops. Development has no role on the operations side, which emphasizes the need for a process that does not need a developer to be available when a system gets released!

▓ **Note** In Figure 8-4 *monitor* is a little special and needs attention. Monitoring any deployment is highly important. Monitoring is the only way of knowing how the system performs. Operations needs to be able to collect metrics, analytics, and a view into the current state. Comprehensive monitoring capabilities should be an acceptance criteria for any deployment!

To summarize this section, supporting a microservices infrastructure requires an automated CI/CD pipeline. It requires investment in tooling, education, and a change of mentality. It is just as important as a strong foundation when constructing a house.

How Does Docker Help?

The previous section discussed CI/CD and DevOps. It spoke about (automated) runbooks. In traditional environments, application servers run and never stop (ideally). Software installations or upgrades are executed on those servers. It is the same process for each supported environment. In addition, developers often need their own, local instance to speed up development without breaking tests or builds that others are running at the same time. It is a huge effort to keep all these servers up and running and configure them all the same way, or, at least, similar to each other.

Docker[7] is a technology that helps simplifying this situation. Docker has the concept of *containers* where a container serves one particular purpose and its content is referred to as *docker image*. Like containers on ships, containers can be stacked and replaced and do not influence others. On the other hand, multiple containers may form one application. Imagine a construction site. Sometimes you'll see containers stacked on top of and next to each other, and each container is different. Although each container serves a different purpose (restroom, office), together they represent a complete construction site management building. Please note that Docker was chosen because it is very popular and because I have personally used it. But it is not the only container solution out there![8]

Having these pictures in mind helps explain why Docker is relevant in the CI/CD, DevOps realm. Figure 8-1 displayed how services run in their own servers. When that figure was discussed, the message was *each service is running in its own server*. With Docker, this changes slightly. There is no server running into which a new service gets deployed. A service brings its own server! Furthermore, containers should be ephemeral, which means they appear and disappear without leaving a trace/ persisting data. Here is an example.

Without Docker: A developer creates a runbook. One area of the runbook explains how to upgrade software within a running application server. Another area explains how to set up a new application server and how to deploy new software into it. The automated runbook may do this without requiring manual effort. However, the new application server and the new software most likely need some sort of configuration, too. To make the complete chain of tasks work, the runbook does not only need to discuss the actual pieces of software; in addition, prerequisites have to be specified to match requirements for the application server and the software within it.

---

[7]Docker, www.docker.com
[8]Docker alternatives, www.1and1.ca/digitalguide/server/know-how/docker-alter
natives-at-a-glance/

With Docker: The story is very different. To launch an application server that includes the desired software, the runbook may only include this line:

```
docker run acme/app:v1.0
```

This is a very simple example but launching docker containers is generally similar. In this case, the application acme/app, version 1.0, will be deployed!

Regardless of the fact that this example is simple, the question is *How does that one statement replace potentially many instructions in a runbook?* To be honest, they are not replaced! But they are executed at a different point in time and by the developers themselves. This is where the automation story becomes relevant again. Here is another example.

I started to work on a project that uses an Apache Tomcat servlet container. Tomcat is open source and can be used for personal or professional use cases. After Tomcat was downloaded, it required a few modifications to adjust it to my personal needs. This is what I would have written into a runbook for the operations team to apply those modifications (shortened, but still many lines):

1. Download Apache Tomcat.

    ```
    https://tomcat.apache.org/download-90.cgi
    ```

2. Install Tomcat at /usr/local/tomcat.

3. Remove the example web applications:

    ```
    rm -rf /usr/local/tomcat/webapps/*
    ```

4. Copy my project into the web applications directory:

    ```
    cp add-ons/web /usr/local/tomcat/webapps/ROOT
    ```

5. ... many more ...

This continues, line by line, until all my requirements have been addressed. If another instance has to be prepared and launched, the same steps have to be executed. It is hopefully obvious that this process is very error prone, especially if executed by a team that does not work with Tomcat in detail. And even if all those lines were moved into a script, the script could still fail!

With Docker, the trick is to run all these instructions when building a *new docker image*! The resulting image is based on a default Tomcat server but includes all my required modifications. This has several advantages:

- Runbooks for operations can be simplified.

- Runbooks reference docker images that are already tested.

- Operations do not need to have any knowledge about Tomcat itself.

Here are the steps that need to be done to get to a simplified runbook that leverages a docker image to run a new container:

1.   Create a new docker image.

2.   Tag the new docker image (provide a useful name).

3.   Push the new image to a repository.

4.   Launch a new container using the new image.

It works like this:

Step 01: Create a new docker image. For that, a so-called dockerfile is required. This file contains the equivalent instructions that were listed in the runbook:

```
# Retrieve a default tomcat server. By default, it is pulled from a public
repository
FROM tomcat:alpine
# remove the default web applications
RUN rm -rf /usr/local/tomcat/webapps/*
# add our own web application
COPY add-ons/web /usr/local/tomcat/webapps/ROOT
# add any other steps that turn the default image into one for your own use
case
```

Step 02: Tag a new docker image. This is like a label that identifies the new image.

```
docker build --tag acme/app:v1.0 .
```

Step 03: Push the new image to a repository. Once the image is pushed it is available to others.

```
docker push <registry>/<username>/acme/app:v1.0
```

As of now, the previous runbook only requires the docker run command from above. The image has certainly been tested and deployed into staging environments beforehand to verify its functionality.

Although this sounds very good and is very good, there are a few differences in comparison to traditional runbook procedures. For me personally, this is the main differentiator:

Containers are *ephemeral*!

This has several implications:

1. Modifications against running containers are lost when the container stops.

   - Containers may even be immutable! With that, modifications would not even be possible!

2. Modifications against containers are valid only as long as they are running.

3. Containers do not persist data by default (which includes configurations).

4. Launching multiple instances are duplicates of each other. Some resources may be available once only (i.e. ports).

5. Each container instance requires the same resources (i.e. memory).

Especially the fact that even configurations are transient may raise the concern of having to build a different image for each configuration. For example, a container in the development environment may access a local database whereas the same container in production connects to a database hosted in a cloud environment.

The concern is valid but gets addressed by launching containers with different configurations. Enabling this is part of the image and is most likely a general requirement. Figure 8-5 illustrates that based on the Tomcat example. Tomcat can be configured through different configuration files. With each environment that launches a container, a different configuration is applied.

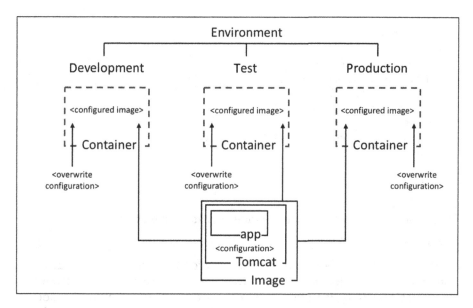

Figure 8-5. Default docker image with an environment-specific configuration for each container

Each environment launches a container using the default docker image. However, each environment applies its own configuration to it. In a real environment, each developer would have its own local configuration. The test configuration would be applied to a build server, or to multiple ones, and one configuration for the production. The docker run command from above would just need another parameter to make this happen. For example, to overwrite the configuration file server.xml, this would be the command:

```
docker run -v dev_server.xml:/usr/local/tomcat/conf/server.xml acme/app:v1.0
```

The local file dev_server.xml would overwrite the file /usr/local/tomcat/conf/server.xml of the Tomcat image.

Docker-compose[9] is another set of tools on top of Docker itself. Docker-compose is helpful in cases where multiple containers have to be launched together, which is most often the case. Here is the content of a docker-compose file (docker-compose.yml) that launches two containers, a load balancer, and a remote cache service:

```
version: '2'
services:
  remote_cache:
    image: memcached
```

---

[9]Docker-compose, https://docs.docker.com/compose/

```
    ports:
      - "11211"
  1b:
    image: dockercloud/haproxy:1.6.7
    environment:
      BALANCE: roundrobin
    restart: always
    volumes:
      - /var/run/docker.sock:/var/run/docker.sock
    links:
      - remote_cache
    ports:
      - 11211:11211
```

The command to launch those containers is as simple as this:

```
docker-compose up
```

After a few seconds those two containers are available. To sum up this section, leveraging Docker has many advantages. However, to run software in Docker at an enterprise scale requires more than just creating the docker images themselves. The infrastructure for that has to be provided, knowledge has to be available, and success and error cases have to be managed just the same way. Platforms such as Red Hat OpenShift[10] or Microsoft Azure for Docker[11] should be evaluated as a Docker management platform.

Summary

Turning an existing monolithic-style application into a microservice architecture is a challenge. This challenge has great benefits but cannot be done without commitment of all teams including business owners. At the end of the transformation, new versions of software systems can be deployed frequently and reduce the risk of failures.

---

[10]Red Hat OpenShift, www.openshift.com
[11]Microsoft Azure for Docker, https://azure.microsoft.com/en-ca/services/kubernetes-service/docker/

Real-Life API Examples

An Elaboration on Publically Available APIs

After discussing API design and implementations, it is time to check out a few existing APIs that are publicly available. Publicly, in most cases, means that a developer account must be created. This is usually free.

These are the APIs for this chapter:

1. Google Maps[1]

2. Microsoft, OpenID Connect[2]

3. IFTTT[3]

The referenced APIs require a different mix of credentials and have very different reasons for their existence. They provide the opportunity to look back at some important aspects that were discussed in this book to close the loop between theory and practice.

---

[1]Google Maps API, https://developers.google.com/maps/documentation/
[2]Microsoft, OpenID Connect, https://docs.microsoft.com/en-us/azure/active-directory/develop/v1-protocols-openid-connect-code
[3]IFTTT, IF This Then That, https://ifttt.com/discover

© CA 2018
S. Preibisch, *API Development*, https://doi.org/10.1007/978-1-4842-4140-0_9

■ **Note**   All information in this chapter is based on official documentation and personal experience and conclusions.

Google Maps

This API enables developers to use Google Maps within their own application. Whenever locations have to be visualized, this API can be used. Free and billed services are available. Without any further ado, the following is an example that can be used from any browser. It will open a map pointing at Vancouver, Canada:

```
https://www.google.com/maps/place/Vancouver,+BC
```

In this context, we care about the structure of the URL (API):

- `https` is the URL scheme.
- `www.google.com` is the server hosting the API.
- `/maps` is the maps service.
- `/place` is the current feature.
- `/Vancouver,+BC` is the location to find.

The API is built in such a way that it starts off globally (`www.google.com`) and each part of the URL path narrows the scope of the location. The API can be compared with to funnel, from wide to narrow.

Embedded Maps

Google provides dedicated APIs that support embedded maps for use within a web site. The documentation is freely accessible; to try them out, a Google account is required. Once the account is created, a so-called API_KEY gets issued. The API_KEY is a unique identifier just for your app!

The documentation provides examples that leverage iFrames. These examples can be copied and pasted into your HTML code and are ready to use. However, we are interested in the API that is used:

```
https://www.google.com/maps/embed/v1/place?key=API_KEY&q=Space+Needle,
Seattle+WA
```

If you look closely, you can find the placeholder API_KEY. Once configured, it will be included in each request. You can also see that the feature has changed from `place` to `embed`. There are even two more selectors: `v1` and `place`. `v1` indicates the version of this API and `place` is referred to as the mode (other values are `search`, `view`, `directions`, and `streetview`).

Figure 9-1 shows a graphical interpretation.

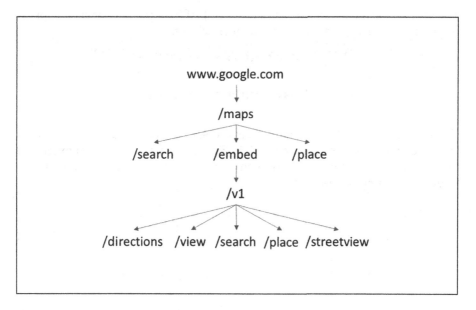

Figure 9-1. Initial graph of Google Maps APIs

Looking at Figure 9-1, at least for me, makes it pretty obvious that it is a challenge to manage a large number of APIs. Imagine v1, v2, v3. In addition, all of these APIs take query parameters that are not the same for all of the mode values. You can see why it is so important to invest design time when starting an API-based environment.

To help users of APIs, Google not only documents the APIs, but it also provides recommendations for securing the API_KEY since it is located within the web site's source code. To prevent anyone else from misusing it, Google has a list of documented and supported ways for mitigating the risk:

- HTTP header "referrer": Provide a list of valid values that Google's server should accept. A request from another location will fail. The value includes your own web server's host name.

- IP address: Provide a list of IP addresses that Google's server should accept. A request from any other IP address will fail.

These supported features are not a guarantee that your API_KEY cannot be misused. In fact, the HTTP header can be added to any request. Nevertheless, it's better than nothing. In addition, the API_KEY can be limited to a set of APIs or just a single one. Trying to access an API that was not listed for this API_KEY will fail.

JavaScript API

The second example, Google's JavaScript (JS) API, supports JavaScript applications. Let's compare the API with one from above:

- JS: https://**maps.googleapis**.com/maps/**api**/js?key =API_KEY

- Embed: https://**www.google**.com/maps/**embed**/v1/ place?key=API_KEY

The JS URL is hosted on a different server. And it has api as a selector in its URL path. If you remember the graph in Figure 9-1 it now needs an extension for yet another level of APIs (and I am sure this only scratches the surface!), as displayed in Figure 9-2.

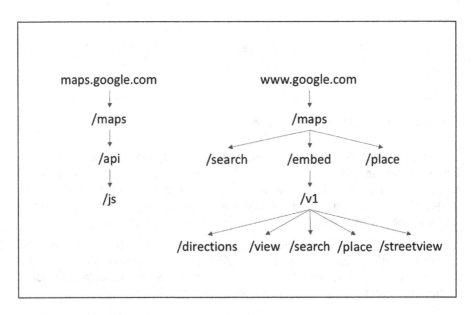

Figure 9-2. Extended graph on Google Maps APIs

The main difference when using those APIs is the level of support developers receive. In one case (embed), the developer needs to construct the correct APIs himself. In the other case (JS), the JS libraries provide helper methods for retrieving data, so only the initial URL has to be configured. If you look into Googles SDKs for supporting iOS and Android, you will find that no URL needs to be configured at all!

If you review Google Maps APIs, you can identify these properties:

- Different levels of access:
  - Anonymously
  - Google account
- Different levels of authentication:
  - None
  - API_KEY
  - OAuth (This was not shown above, but Google also supports OAuth as an authorization scheme for mobile applications.)
- Different levels of support for developers:
  - None (documentation only) for embed scenarios.
  - JavaScript: Only one URL needs to be configured.
  - SDKs: URLs are completely hidden.
- Hierarchical URL path

Whenever your organization wants to start an API-based system, check that the relevant properties from above have been addressed. They are not only relevant for Google Maps but for any API. If there are any plans of monetizing APIs, some kind of authentication is required.

In addition, the process of onboarding developers has to be designed. Developers do not simply appear out of nowhere; they need an easy way to join the system. In Google's case, one account works for all of its services, which makes it very easy to get started! And getting started is done by one sign-up process only!

Microsoft, OpenID Connect

Microsoft is one of the main drivers for OpenID Connect and one of the early supporters. Since OpenID Connect is an identity layer, it is certainly only useful in a context that requires knowledge about users (or resource_owners in OAuth terms). For that, any interaction with Microsoft's OpenID Connect implementation requires a Microsoft account such as myname@hotmail.com. Microsoft's services are also used with Microsoft Office 365. As for Google, the documentation is publicly available, but an account is required to use the APIs.

OpenID Connect Discovery

As specified in OpenID Connect, Microsoft supports the Discovery endpoint, which can simply be called from a browser:

`https://login.microsoftonline.com/common/.well-known/ openid-configuration`

It returns a JSON document describing the APIs, OAuth SCOPEs, and other values that help developers build an application.

The URL contains the default URL path, which is the same for all OpenID Connect-supporting providers: `/.well-known/openid-configuration`. It is a reminder that it's nice to adhere to standards!

However, since we care about APIs, let's look at the structure of it:

- `https` is the URL scheme.
- `login.microsoftonline.com` is the server hosting the API.
- `/common` is the tenant.
- `/.well-known/openid-configuration` is the discovery document location.

The interesting component here is common, representing a tenant. Microsoft's online services are available as SaaS[4] and therefore they are multi-tenant–enabled. This means that anyone, after creating an account, can start leveraging OpenID Connect features for his own purposes. The value common represents the general tenant. For example, if you sign up with an email address, that will be handled as tenant common. However, if you sign up with an email address and create your own user directory, you also get your own tenantId tied to your own user directory. To reference a tenant, the value common is replaced with {tenant}.

Microsoft has chosen to require the tenant in more or less all APIs. For example, the OAuth endpoints, such as /authorize and /token, include the tenantId as well:

`https://login.microsoftonline.com/{tenant}/oauth2/authorize`

With that, the OpenID Connect Discovery document is tailored to each tenant.

---

[4]SaaS, Software as a Service, https://en.wikipedia.org/wiki/Software_as_a_service

id_token Validation

The value for tenant is also included in responses. For example, an id_token will always include the value `tid` (tenant). The concept of tenant is similar to a namespace. This becomes especially valuable when validating id_token. The validation can be used to identify different groups of users, such as your own users, users of partners, and unknown users. A typical validation could have this logic:

```
IF ( validate(id_token) == valid ) THEN
IF ( tid == my_own_tid )
        THEN grant access to internal, partner and public documentation;
ELSE IF ( tid == partner_tid )
        THEN grant access to partner and public documentation
ELSE grant access to public documentation
```

Once everything is tied to a tenant, it is simple to create different virtual spaces. For each one, different experiences can be supported. Figure 9-3 visualizes this.

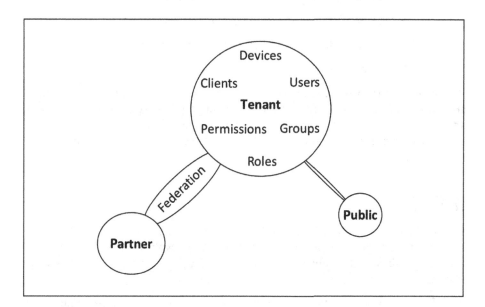

Figure 9-3. Virtual spaces

Whatever is configured in the virtual space of the tenant (Figure 9-3) can be extended (with limitations) to partners using simple federation mechanisms. The public space can also be served by restricting users of that space even more.

For example, software developers usually maintain internal documents that include functional specifications and test results for features they are implementing. Since these documents are meant for internal users only, they never get published. Nevertheless, sometimes partners could be more effective if they had at least read-access to those documents. Using OpenID Connect, OAuth-protected APIs, and the concept of tenants could support the use case where partners log in to the internal system but only get read-access to these technical documents.

If you review Microsoft's OpenID Connect implementation, you can identify these properties:

- Different levels of access:
  - Anonymously
  - Microsoft account
- Different levels of authentication:
  - OAuth for applications (secrets and pki)
  - User authentications via username, password
  - Support for MFA (multi-factor authentication)
- Multi-tenancy

Whenever your organization wants to provide a SaaS for authentication and authorizations, make sure the relevant properties from above have been addressed. Multi-tenancy especially has to be part of early designs. Trying to add that kind of requirement into a ready-to-use single-tenant system is a very intense process.

IFTTT

Google Maps and Microsoft OpenID Connect are services that can be leveraged by developers. Anyone can start developing against their APIs immediately. IFTTT is slightly different. If you haven't worked with IFTTT, this is what is does.

IFTTT is a SaaS that hosts applications. Users may combine these applications to implement message flows that follow the pattern "IF <something happens> THEN do <this or that>." For example, having API- and cloud-enabled lights (e.g. Philips Hue) and cameras (e.g. Netgear Arlo) enable flows such as "**IF** my camera detects motion **THEN** turn on my front door light." For end users specifically, this is done by simply configuring a few dialogs on a web site or mobile app.

If your company wants to become "the lights" or "the camera" provider, you need to provide APIs! IFTTT needs APIs to connect to! Your company needs to become an API provider!·

Authentication and Authorization

IFTTT accepts different authentication and authorization methods. We care about OAuth, which is one of the options. Based on the lights and camera example, Figure 9-4 gives an overview how everything connects to each other.

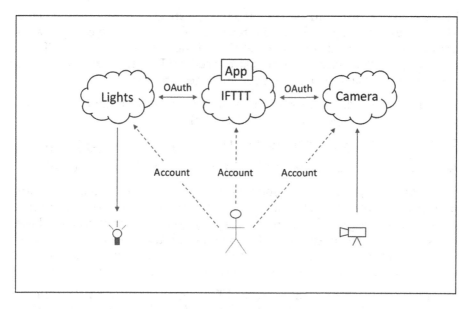

Figure 9-4. Overview of connections between components in IFTTT

In IFTTT a user can pick and choose features he wants to use. One feature could be "turn lights on" and the other could be "notify me when my camera detects motion." To support this, IFTTT needs to be able to communicate with each of those systems. In Figure 9-4, OAuth is emphasized. This is because OAuth can authenticate users and collect users' authorization decisions. If you are the vendor of the camera system, your system needs to support OAuth as a server! In addition, your server also needs to support an IFTTT API Key.

Let's have a look how IFTTT APIs are structured. IFTTT provides test endpoints that are, more or less, always the same. And there are application-specific endpoints.

This is the test API: `https://{your-server}/ifttt/v1/test/setup`

- `https` is the URL scheme.
- `your-server` is your server, hosting the test API.
- `/ifttt` is the indicator of the platform.
- `/v1` is the API version.
- `/test` is the feature.
- `/setup` is the test step.

You may notice that `your-server` is shown, instead of having some kind of `itfttt-server` location! This indicates that IFTTT is communicating as a client only. And, in fact, that is the case! What is not shown here is that IFTTT test requests always include an API_KEY called `IFTTT-Service-Key`. This has to be supported and validated in your implementation, too!

Here are more APIs for triggers and actions (two different entities in IFTTT of which you may implement both or just one):

Trigger: `https://{your-server}/ifttt/v1/triggers/{your-trigger}`

Action: `https://{your-server}/ifttt/v1/actions/{your-action}`

The APIs' URL paths end on `your-trigger` and `your-action`. Regardless of it saying `your-*`, it is still dictated by the platform. That path element is derived from a trigger or action that you may have implemented. What I like is that there are no questions like *How shall I name it?* It follows a pattern that makes everyone's life easy. And, in the end, it does not really matter how it's called as long as it makes sense in association with a supported feature.

From a developer's point of view, IFTTT has made it very comfortable to work within their website and to test and verify implementations as a client. Here are the highlights:

- Easy-to-use web interface:
  - Easy on-boarding for new developers
- Easy-to-use test framework
  - Developers are well supported during their implementation phase
- Comprehensive documentation
  - Practically all needed topics are documented online
- Easy user experience
  - End users are able to configure an app within minutes with just a few clicks

If your company is in the process of providing a platform for similar features, check out IFTT, which I think is a very good example of a well-designed system.

What to Remember Based on These Examples

Here is what you should remember based on what has been discussed here:

- Support flexible authentication and authorization schemes.
- Plan for free and billable APIs or features of APIs.
- Provide comprehensive but well-structured public documentation.
- Plan for multitenancy as of the first design sessions (if needed).
- Provide easy onboarding methods for developers and users.
- Enable partners with privileged access.

Anyone following these guide lines should have a good starting point!

Summary

The discussed APIs serve different purposes, they use different authentication and authorization schemes, and they also monetize their APIs differently. However, they are examples of well-designed systems with an ecosystem that makes it easy for any developer to get involved.

If your company is in the process of starting an API-driven business, it is highly important to look at the whole system: APIs, documentation, accessibility to the system, presentation, features, and usability from different audiences. APIs do not get popular by just existing!

Key Terms

Provided here are full spellings of acronyms and brief definitions that will be of use to you as you read the book.

Term	Description
access_token	A temporary token that provides access to OAuth-protected APIs
API	Application Programming Interface. In the context of this book, they are mainly REST –based
API Key	An identifier of an application presented at an API
API management	A reference to all aspects of an API development environment: API developer onboarding, API documentation, API monetization, and API implementation as well as API lifecycle
CI/CD	Continuous Integration/Continuous Deployment
Contract first	Starting the API development based on documentation rather than an implementation
CORBA	Common Object Request Broker Architecture
CSR	Certificate Signing Request
Docker	A container platform
Docker image	The source for a Docker container
ESB	Enterprise Service Bus
FAPI	Financial-grade API. A working group in the context of the OpenID Foundation
FIPS	Federal Information Processing Standards

(*continued*)

© CA 2018

S. Preibisch, *API Development*, https://doi.org/10.1007/978-1-4842-4140-0

Term	Description
ICAP	Internet Content Adaptation Protocol. An interface used to, for example, request a virus scan via an API call
IDP	Identity provider. A source of identities
IIW	Internet Identity Workshop. The place where OAuth 2.0 and OpenID Connect were initiated
JWE	JSON Web Encryption
JWKS	JSON Web Key Set. A list of public keys used to verify a JWS
JWS	JSON Web Signature
JWT	JSON Web Token. A JSON-based message format supporting digital signatures and encryption
LDAP	Lightweight Access Directory Protocol
Let's Encrypt	A free service for issuing SSL certificates
Microservice	A term found in the context of microservice architecture. An API (microservice) serving one purpose only
Mobile first	An approach of supporting mobile use cases and mobile users first
MVP	Minimum viable product. A version of a product that supports the least number of features that are required to make it usable
NFC	Near-field communication
NIST	National Institute of Standards and Technology
OAuth 2.0	An authorization framework. It uses different types of tokens to provide access to OAuth-protected APIs
Omnipresence	Being represented on multiple platforms at the same time
OTP	One-time password
PCI	Payment Card Industries. Also PCI DSS, Payment Card Industry Data Security Standard
PSD2	Payment Service Directive 2. A European law to force banks to provide API access to accounts
QA	Quality assurance
RESTFul	Representational State Transfer
RFC	Request For Comment. In the context of this book, RFC 6749, 7515, 7519
Roadmap	An indication of features planned for the near future
SAML	Security Assertion Markup Language. A XML-based message format used for authentication and authorizations
SCOPE (OAuth)	A list of values representing permissions in the context of OAuth

(continued)

Term	Description
SLA	Service-level agreement
SOAP	Simple Object Access Protocol. An XML-based message format for exchanging data
Social login	The process of authenticating users by their username provided by a social platform
Step-up authentication	Requiring an authentication method that indicates a higher trust than a previous authentication mechanism
Swagger	A machine-readable document describing an API definition
TLS	Transport Layer Security
WADL	Web Application Description Language
WAF	Web application firewall
WSDL	Web Service Description Language
YAML	YAML Ain't Markup Language. A clear text message format, usually used for configurations

Index

© CA 2018
S. Preibisch, *API Development*, https://doi.org/10.1007/978-1-4842-4140-0

Printed in the United States
By Bookmasters